Queer Paganism:
Spirituality that Embraces All Identities

Jo Green

DEDICATION

This book is dedicated to Angela, who taught me everything I know.

CONTENTS

ACKNOWLEDGMENTS

I'd like to acknowledge the various people who've made this book a reality, my lovely wife Angela Green who supported me throughout and Maeve Devine for her inspiration in getting this book from an idea to a reality. To the countless friends who've supported me in the writing. Without your help, patience and hours spent listening to me harp on about it, thank you. You are all magickal beings made of light. .

FOREWORD

There are many books about Paganism available, written from American and European perspectives. Each book will be written from the authors own understanding and spiritual practices. This book is no different.

Heavily influenced by spending most of my formative spiritual years in South Africa, a lot of books didn't adequately address the needs of the South African person who is interested in Paganism. The Eurocentric, northern hemisphere centric writings didn't apply to the culture or even the world view of South Africa; for example, even the seasons, festivals and cardinal points are differently applicable to the southern hemisphere.

South Africa is very far from the Western world, both geographically and spiritually. Our spiritual influences have been shaped by our environments. The African Traditional Religions, our cultures, our family structures, our upbringing, the apartheid era, the struggle for freedom and the achieving of a peaceful democracy have all brought me to a personal philosophy where, whatever your views and your background, you have a right to be respected, a right to be heard and a right to have an opinion. The influences lead me to a path that was created and written based on research across various paths, logic, critical thinking and quite a bit of intuition. That is what this book reflects; it's a mixture of personal experiences, beliefs and practices with the beliefs and practices of other people, with just a dash of pure pagan or Wiccan theory. This being said, the structure of our beliefs follows a Wiccan basis, however our practices are more 'Wiccan-ish' than strictly Wiccan.

This book is also heavily influenced by my experiences of differencing gender. The author is on the trans spectrum, and this book hopes to be inclusive of all gender expression and identity and looks to show how a different, less binary view of gender applies in paganism, magick and witchcraft.

That doesn't mean it isn't applicable to anyone who is cisgender or not based in South Africa, far from it. These intersectional experiences of being different have actually allowed me to develop a magickal system and a world view that is open minded, has more explanation and reasoning to it than what we've experienced before. My approach will allow you to learn what the theories are, without the need for dogmatic compliance. I (hopefully) teach you what you need to know, and empower you to think for yourself.

JO GREEN

Section 1:
Introduction to Queer Paganism

JO GREEN

1. QUEER PAGAN MANIFESTO

Queer paganism is exactly that, paganism for queers. This book aims to cut through the binary to give you a living breathing working way of life that allows queers to progress on their own quests for meaning in an inclusive way.

Unlike many pagan and Wiccan teachers, I don't claim to have any lineage other than my own spiritual practice. I've constructed a philosophy and spirituality using some of the best ideas from old and new pagan thinking, but disregarded the parts that are problematic or just too constrictive to be able to work with.

This book is written for all self-identified queers who are looking for spirituality that is open, accepting and sympathetic to the needs of the modern queer.

WHAT IS QUEER?

Self-definition is going through a revival at the moment; we're all searching for the words we use to define ourselves and as such the meanings of these definitions are constantly changing. For that reason it makes sense to define what this book means by queer.

Queer is anyone who is outside of the norm and encompasses a broad range of identities that don't quite fit. Queer is inclusive of Lesbian, Gay, Bisexual, Asexual, Graysexual, Pansexual, Intersex, Trans, Agender,

Cisgender and open-minded straight people. Queer is a self-identification that allows anyone who feels like the conservative, straight, heteronormative model doesn't fit them.

Each and every person experiences their identity differently. We all see out world through our own eyes, we can also therefor choose to accept and reject those societally imposed definitions if we choose to. If you reject what has been attributed to you by society, in my book, you are queer. Welcome to the family.

WHAT IS PAGANISM?

Paganism is the rebirth of the old ways, from times before the spread of organised religions, for example Christianity and the Crusades. Pagans follow the beliefs and practices adhered to by simple folk and generally have the following in common:
- Pagans respect nature and everything in it
- They believe in magick, but not all practice magick
- They believe that balance is important
- They often believe in a masculine and a feminine aspect to deity (this may be angels, faeries, Gods, Goddesses, etc.). Deity is literally translated as Divine Nature. It is used to refer to gods, goddesses and other divine beings. There is an increasing belief in non-gendered deity (for example a universal spirit, totem animals or gods and goddesses who either have both (for example Baphomet) or change their gender (Loki))

Paganism, also referred to as Neo-paganism, as a whole is generally a nature based religion with certain characteristics as for example, devotion to multiple deities (also known as polytheism), a respect for nature, belief in magick and sometimes the belief in reincarnation. Strictly speaking it is classified as someone who does not follow Christianity, Islam or Judaism. Paganism comes from the Latin Paganus, meaning country dweller, and was used to describe the people who still practiced the old ways as they lived outside of the main centres and cities. Therefore, they had not been influenced by the more influential religions of the time for example Christianity, Judaism, Islam etc. which had more of a stronghold in the cities.

Today, Paganism is the all-encompassing word used for all the old religions, for example the ancient Roman and Greek religions. What is used today is called Neo-paganism by academics, however, this word is often disregarded by pagans, as they feel it lacks the authority that following the old religion has. Using either Paganism or Neo-Paganism is acceptable, it's about how you choose to self-identify.

The main difficulty of defining paganism is that paganism can be seen as an umbrella that may or may not cover many religions. In truth a combination of various definitions will lead you somewhere closer to what Paganism is. It's also used as a form of self-identification, which means that it's very open to interpretation by individuals, which causes the word's meaning to change over time.

Although most of these will apply to most pagans, this does not mean that you are not a pagan if you don't believe all of these tenets. For example, most practitioners of High Magick (Golden Dawn, Crowley, and OTO) do not worship deity in the more common sense of worship, they believe they ascend to godhood while practicing their rituals, they are generally not nature based, but they do fall under the Pagan umbrella.

THE EARLY ROOTS OF PAGANISM

To find the history of paganism, one would have to take an anthropological view of humankind. Back in the history of humans, before science, people lived in an uncertain world where one was never sure if the sun would come up and when it got cold, if the warm weather would return allowing for the animals to return so that hunting could continue or later, the growing of crops. These early people would turn to a knowledgeable one within the tribe, and this person would find explanations and assurances. The person who was knowledgeable at the time would have been a Shaman or a priest figure. This is also where many rituals were initiated, for example to do a rain dance to bring rain when it is dry, but also the rituals of giving back to deity, the earth etc. after a good harvest. This knowledgeable person would later be called a medicine man, a shaman, a witchdoctor, a druid, a sangoma etc. This is where paganism started. Over time the wise one also fulfilled the roles of a spiritual leader, a healer, a mystic and counsellor to both the leaders of the tribe and the common people. This is also where we see the beginnings of mythical people such as Merlin.

As human development progressed, the explanations and abilities and systems of belief progressed and became more sophisticated. The rituals, deities, practices and beliefs also evolved into the complex structures that we see today, where we have mixed myth with science to form new belief systems.

Below is a list of the more common forms of Paganism found today, however there are many more forms of paganism being practiced:

- Traditionalist Wicca:
    - Gardnerian Wicca – Wicca practiced according to the Gardnerian principles & practises
    - Alexandrian Wicca – Wicca practiced by those following Alex Sanders
    - Dianic Wicca – Wicca where the Goddess Diana is worshipped exclusively
    - Eclectic Wicca: This is anyone who practices Wicca that does not base their practice on a formalised tradition for example
    - Solitary Wicca
    - School of Wicca (online)
- Norse paganism (also known as Germanic paganism) based on Norse mythologies
    - Asatru
    - Viking
    - Odinism
- Celtic Paganism: based on the British mythologies
    - Druidism
    - Celtic Shamanism
    - Grail based Wicca
    - Faery Wicca
    - Welsh
    - Anglo Saxon
    - Scottish
    - Irish
- High Magick:
    - Babylonian
    - Sumerian
    - Egyptian High Magick
    - Kabballah
- Shamanism – Where one is an intermediary between the natural and spiritual world, who travels between worlds in a trance state, and while in trance communes with the spiritual world to make changes in the natural world.
    - Native American (North and South American)
    - Celtic

- African (sangoma, inyanga)
- Aboriginal
- Himalayans
- Icelandic

PAGANISM, WICCA OR WITCHCRAFT?

In this book you can expect the explanations to apply to Paganism as a whole, yet much of the common pagan practices today stem from Gerald Gardner and Wicca. Wicca is a pagan religion, but Paganism is not the same as Wicca.

Wicca is the religious system that was founded principally by Gerald Brosseau Gardner (1884-1964) and the writings of Aleister Crowley (1875-1947). Gerald Garner drew on works and histories of the pre-Christian religions of England and other parts of the world, his claims that Wicca was purely a re-emergence of the 'old ways', has been disproved by historians and theologians alike. Wicca has a lot of structure to the religion, structure which although useful when starting out, can also bind people to believing that there is only one true way to be a Wiccan (which is of course not true).

This brings us to the topic of witchcraft. There seems to be much debate on what witchcraft is and is not. Witchcraft can be understood as literally the craft of a witch. A craft by its nature is to create something. Witchcraft is the performing of spells, making of potions, creams, oils, candles etc. using the magical and natural knowledge of the things that you use. Thus a large company making commercial soap in not practicing witchcraft, the little old lady down the road who makes soaps to cure you of bad skin or to improve your luck is practicing a form of witchcraft, irrespective of her religion. On the other hand, Wicca is a religion that has members who may or may not practice witchcraft. Gardner started off Wicca, since then there have been many offshoots, such as Celtic, Asatru etc. which have more eclectic set of beliefs and practices.

This can be summarised as saying that Witchcraft is a practice of creating something using magickal knowledge whereas, Wicca is a religion. Wicca and Witchcraft are not and should not be classified as the same thing. Paganism is the umbrella term encompassing many non-traditional beliefs (including Wicca and the use of witchcraft).

2. A SPIRITUALITY THAT EMBRACES ALL IDENTITIES

Spirituality is a way to give life meaning. It's a way to explain some of the unexplainable events in life and a way to find comfort. It's also a journey of self-discovery. The purpose of a spiritual journey should be to learn and develop yourself, a way to be able to identify who you are and how you fit into the world at large. It can be a way to find community and a way to embrace the things about you that you previously may have thought of as shameful or secret. How then, in this search for self-definition and self-acceptance can a religion deny people who choose not to fall into the norms of society when it was the journey itself that lead them to those conclusions?

The restrictions that religions place on people are not placed by the religions, but rather by people, and thus, if we as people reject those definitions placed on by the outside world (be that by religions, governments, schools, parents etc.) we have a legitimate right to do so.

PAGANISM AND GENDER

A core difference in paganism and the key that drew me to it in the start of my journey is the acknowledgement and celebration of duality. Pagan belief is centred on balance between good and evil, light and dark, day and night and importantly masculine and feminine. There is an acknowledgement of the feminine and masculine divine; there should not be a single male god, but also a balancing female goddess.

In most pagan teachings everything can be classified into neat polarities of positive and negative, sending and receiving energy, masculine and feminine. The principles behind how this classification is done are often based on whether the item being represented was phallic-shaped (for male) or receptacle shaped (for female). The energy classifications were often based on projecting being male (representing the male sperm projecting outwards from the body) and the receptive being female (based on the womb). This classification then further sought to classify based on traditionally feminine and masculine characteristics (warm and nurturing for female and cold and decisive for male). The theory behind the polarities is that these opposing forces create a tension, and in this tension the magick is found. While this neat, clear classification was very useful to remember when starting out, I found that the deeper I delved into what this meant to my own personal spiritual practices, the harder it was for me to accept.

Part of the problem was also that this classification was too heavily reliant on the heteronormative standard of relationships and sex. With the idea that the two polarities were always masculine and feminine, came the implied regulation that it was only by having a representative of both polarities could you achieve balance (every god requires a goddess and thus by inference every priestess requires a priest). When addressed, there were a few well-meaning but ultimately misinformed teachers who advised that two women in a relationship would be able to conduct a ritual together if the 'butch' one took on the male aspect 'because that's the role they play in relationship anyway' and the same would apply to more feminine gay men (who would presumably take on the role feminine aspect of the divine).

A bigger part of the problem was that my own identity didn't fit into the neat gender classifications of male and female, while I had no language to describe it at the time. I had a deep sense of unease with being classified as either specifically female or specifically male. I'm still not especially happy with labels, however I'm happier with genderqueer, non-binary or demi-feminine than I am with cis female/woman. Also being in a relationship with a trans woman, any fixed ideas of being neatly binary male or female (and all the associated physical and reproductive emphasis) were at a complete juxtaposition to what I knew to be true.

So how do I reconcile this binary language and worldview of the teaching s of paganism with my own? This took me years to completely figure out and come to terms with. What follows in this book is what my wife and I developed over time and with much dismantling and revising of old views and teachings to fit into a more open accepting and all-embracing worldview.

RECONCILING THE BINARY

It's often explained that everywhere in nature, the concepts of masculine and feminine come to the fore. Plants, animals and people are either male or female. Some plants for instance have a male plant and a female plant; the male plant creates the seed, while the female plant bears the fruit. Most flowers also have a male (stamen) and female (carpel) part on them. The stamen contains the pollen. Either through wind pollination or from insects, the pollen travels to the carpel of the flower, or a different flower. This fertilises the flower, and the plant bears fruit containing the seed.

Other objects also have these associations; the sun is seen as masculine, and the moon feminine. It is explained that the sun has a direct effect on all life on earth, and is thus masculine while the moon's affects are subtle, controlling the tides, and the gravitational forces of the planet earth. Both are equally necessary and the feminine focus means that often the moon is emphasised.

This binary split is often also ascribed to emotions; masculinity is often seen as intellect, ambition, drive, energy, determination, practicality etc. whereas female is seen as nurturing, spirituality, creativity, love, emotions, intuition etc. Masculine is a force that pushes whereas feminine force pulls, and this association is often used when doing magick. Masculine force is used to drive something out of your life, but feminine for to create something or draw something towards you.

For a queer perspective, rather than seeing things as masculine and feminine use the electrical charges. Things can be negatively charged (have an excess of electrons), positively charged (have a lack of electrons) or neutral (have a balance between the protons and electrons). This analogy can also be used to see the negative charge as masculine (as the electrons moving around denote the sperm) and the positive charge as feminine (which in terms of protons are the neutralising force attracting the electrons). But the ideal is neutral. The neutral represents balance, being overtly negative/masculine or positive/feminine while it can generate electricity, is not ideal for stability. The only reason why electricity is created is the forces of positive and negative attract each other with the ultimate aim of creating balance.

This doesn't mean that we see one as greater than the other, or that it is bad to be overtly feminine or masculine, but rather that the key to enlightenment is actually to find balance.

The use of masculine and feminine is merely representative, we can all find examples where the traits assigned to masculine and feminine don't apply. Not all women are emotional and not all men are ambitious. You can, in your magickal and spiritual practice choose to ignore the masculine and feminine and treat them as purely polarities or negative and positive, or you can recognise that these descriptions and associations which applied to a specific people at a specific time. And where the associations don't work for you, change them. The great gift of paganism is that this is your spirituality, you are in charge and you get to define how the rules work. You are the one working with the energy; you get to decide what is right for you.

3. DEITY

Very little of the detailed truth of any of the pre-Christian deities exists without the filter of the authors. During the 19th century science was rising in popularity and mythologies were seen as outdated thinking of primitive people. Even those documenting the mythologies of ancient people were sceptical of its use. Even James George Frazer (1854–1941), who wrote one of the most revered books on ancient Greek and Roman mythologies The Golden Bough was disdainful of the importance of ritual and mythology for people. He is quoted as saying that human development of *"the higher thought... has on the whole been from magic through religion to science"* (Frazer, 1922).

There was also no single form of worship or doctrine for many of the deities as the practices varied between places as well as over time. In the same way that different people and groups view the Christian god differently (some attributing punishment and vengeance, some attributing kindness and paternity, some attributing all of these aspects), the people that did (and still do) worship or work with deities select the aspects of the deity that best suits their circumstances and their needs.

Your relationship with the divine is a personal one. No information; not even the information contained here can be denoted as being the absolute truth. Choosing to include deity in your spiritual practice is ultimately a personal choice. Many choose to use deity in ritual because they find it simpler to use a focus and it becomes part of the magick. They key is to explore the mythologies that interest you. Find the deity that best suits your character, your understanding and your worldview.

THE PSYCHOLOGY OF WORKING WITH DEITY

The initial disdain for mythology was what piqued the interest of Carl G. Jung (1875 - 1961). He was a Swiss psychiatrist who worked closely with Sigmund Freud (1856 - 1939) the so-called father of Psychoanalytic theory. Jung studied mythologies to understand their purpose for humans. To see how Jung explains the purpose of mythology, you first need some background into his theory of the human mind.

Jung's theory of the structure of the human personality states that a person has the conscious mind, the personal unconscious and the collective unconscious. The conscious mind is the part of your mind that you are aware of. These are the decisions and choices you make, and your rational thought. The conscious mind is what you are aware of and what you perceive about yourself and your relationship with your environment. Think of the mind as an iceberg, the small part that is visible above the water is the conscious mind. The huge part below the water is the unconscious mind.

The unconscious is the part of your mind that you are not aware of. The personal unconscious is the part of your mind that you are not aware of that exists for you alone. It is also often referred to as your sub-conscious. The personal unconscious is like a sponge. Images, thoughts and information are absorbed into the personal unconscious, without the filter of the conscious mind. The personal unconscious affects your conscious mind in subtle ways. For example, you are waiting to cross the road at a busy intersection. You are concentrating on when it will be safe to cross the road, so your conscious mind shuts out everything but what you are concentrating on. A while later, you realise that you have a song playing over and over in your mind and you don't remember hearing it anywhere. This is probably the effect of information from the personal unconscious rising to the surface of your conscious mind. This is because while your conscious mind has shut out everything except the crossing the road safely, your personal unconscious mind absorbs everything you've seen, heard, felt, tasted and smelled.

Information can move from the conscious to the subconscious mind and from the subconscious to the conscious mind. The difference is how it is accessed. The information in the conscious is freely available, whereas the information from the subconscious cannot be accessed through conscious thought. Information in the subconscious can be accessed through hypnosis, meditation and dreaming.

Jung describes the collective unconscious as an unchanging collection of information that is the same among all people. Information contained in the collective unconscious is common among all people, for example symbols, signs, associations and archetypes. Archetypes can be seen as the basis for mythology and pagan pantheons.

Archetypes are very difficult to explain, but very easy to understand. An archetype is the first original model upon which all other ideas are built. For example, the following are some, but by no means all, archetypes that are found in mythology:

- The Great Father (e.g. Uranus, Zeus, Osiris)
- The Great Mother (e.g. Cerridwen, Demeter, Isis)
- The Virgin Huntress (e.g. Artemis, Diana, Atlanta)
- The Hunter God (e.g. Apollo, Orion, Mabon)
- The Triple Goddess (Maiden, Mother, Crone) (e.g. Hecate, Holle, Brigid)
- The Trickster (e.g. Loki, Crow, Anansi)

What this means is that we all can identify with some archetypes in mythology. This does not make deity any more or less real than they are to you. What you need to do is choose a pantheon that you can identify with and then research the Gods and Goddesses, until you find ones you like and then use that deity concept when you do ritual.

THE WAY MAGICK WORKS FOR ME

I've always been a sceptic, I was sceptical of organised religion, sceptical of mainstream schooling and sceptical of anything that relied on me taking someone else's word for it. Unless I was given a good rational reason for the 'why' of things, I wouldn't believe them. This was one of the things that first attracted me to paganism and to its magickal system.

The way I see it, magick works because you use it to focus. It's a way to set your mind on a path which will ultimately open you up to opportunities that may have been there all along, but you may not have necessarily looked at them before. The act of thinking about making a decision to cast a spell starts the process, it enables you to formulate what you want in your mind and then, as you start gathering all the things you need for a spell, you start weighing up the options and making minuscule decisions about what form you want the spell to take and what you want your future to look like.

In order to explain how magick works however, I've drawn from some science, some pagan thinking and some of my own experiences. I think whatever you take away from this is that magick works, as long as you believe it works. If you can't get your head around it at all, no amount of crystals or incense or oils will be able to make it work for you. You are the key to any spell or belief system that exists. You are the catalyst, you make it all happen.

DEMYSTIFYING ENERGY

The foundation of the belief system and the magick that we practice is energy. This foundation allows us to bring all pagan systems together. Without this basic knowledge any magick or ritual that you will do will end up being meaningless in the greater sense.

What is Energy? Energy is the stuff that everything is made of, the stuff that connects us all.

At the highest level all things are differentiated as being made up of cells. These cells are made up of elements on the periodic table, at a level below that, all elements are made up of atoms, namely protons, electrons and neutrons. These protons, electrons and neutrons are made up of much smaller particles (sub atomic particles) and then sub-atomic particles are made of something else, and down and down it goes. Now this is where the science and energy working are the same, all matter (energy) vibrates which then takes on some form that can be seen, tasted, felt, smelt or heard. With the right tools all matter can be rearranged to take on another form. Scientists have been doing this for years using their tools of the trade, so can we. But we use the most powerful tool, our mind. This essence is energy.

Many people believe that they cannot work with energy as they cannot feel it or sense it. This is a great misconception as all people can sense energy and do every day without any hindrances. If everything is made up of energy it then follows that we see, hear, taste and feel energy every day. Light is a form of energy; heat is a form of energy. Energy is everywhere and it can be sensed using one or more of your senses. A simple example is a lit candle; you can see the light, feel the heat, smell the wax, hear the crackle or even taste the wax (not recommended).

According to Einstein, *"Energy cannot be created or destroyed; it can only be changed from one form to another"*. So in the above example we can see how the potential energy of the candle wick is transferred into heat and light energy.

In a similar sense, we cannot create energy, but there are various ways to tap into boundless amounts of energy. This is called raising energy, that can be used for a specific purpose e.g. Healing, magick, ritual etc. This is discussed further on in the chapter.

Some people sense energy using touch, for example a tingly sensation or pressure against the skin, other people can see energy, for example auras, some people hear energy as a whooshing sound, while some can smell or even taste energy. Then there are those few people that are so sensitive that they seem to have supernatural powers.

EXTRA SENSORY PERCEPTION AND PSYCHOKINESIS

Extra sensory perception is the use of non-regular (paranormal) senses. Paranormal is literally translated to outside of the normal. Generally used to describe ghosts, hauntings etc. It's also used in reference to cryptozoology (the study of hidden animals, for example the Loch Ness monster, yetis and Bigfoot). Psychokinesis is the active or sending of information or psychic phenomena. The difference is the person who is expending active or passive in the interaction, extra sensory perception is the active receiving or sensing of information that shouldn't (in theory) be possible, and the sender would be passive. Whereas psychokinesis involves the psychic force being actively sent out and the receiver would passively receive the force or message.

Types of Extra Sensory Perception
- Clairvoyance, or Remote Viewing - the ability to sense or 'see' (non-physically) distant objects, places, and people. Individuals who see ghosts and spirits are probably clairvoyant.
- Clairaudience, or remote hearing - the 'hearing' of paranormal information.
- Astral Projection (OOBE) or Travelling Clairvoyance - Full experience at a remote location while the physical body sleeps.
- Psychometry - the reading of information by the touch of physical objects.
- Telepathic receiver - the ability to directly receive thought (communication) at a distance, with no physical connection to the sender. There are many everyday examples of this, in which we think something just as another person is about to say it. This is an easy one to test for through experiment. Very dramatic cases of telepathy have been recorded; there is often an emotional element in such cases.

- A 'channel' or medium, as in a séance, who is in direct communication with a 'spirit' or entity.
- Experience with an Ouija board, pendulum, or automatic writing.
- Precognition - to foresee the future. Again, highly emotional events are the ones most likely to be 'tuned in'.
- Retrocognition - knowledge of the past, by paranormal means.

Types of Psychokinesis
- Telepathic sender - the transmitter in the telepathy just discussed.
- Psychokinesis (or telekinesis) proper - the ability to move objects by means of psychic force. Somewhat along the same lines are poltergeist (noisy ghost) phenomena in which objects move of their own accord or noises are heard. There is always a human agent involved - frequently a teenage girl - who appears to be the source of psychic energy.
- Psychic healing - the ability to heal various illnesses and infirmities. There are many documented cases of this. Usually it involves a healer and a subject, although there are recent cases involving cancer patients learning to heal themselves.
- Teleportation, apportation, and levitation.

Section 2:
Magick

4. THE NATURE OF MAGICK

Aleister Crowley defines magick as *"the Science and Art of causing Change to occur in conformity with will"*. (Crowley, Desti, & Waddell, Magick: Liber Aba, 1998)

Magick is the precursor to science. We used the effects of science before we knew that it is possible through sheer faith. When we use magick, we believe (with little or no solid proof) that the universe works in a certain way, and thus based on our beliefs, we can manipulate things in the universe to conform to our will.

Think of it this way, there may have people who could make a metal object move by sheer force of will. Perhaps it is so, but perhaps it is a hoax using a magnet to move this metal object. To the unschooled masses, this may have been seen as powerful magick, but to the person, it would just be the way that certain objects interact; some objects are attracted to other objects. Now, in the twenty first century, magnetism is old news, everyone knows about it and that it works, it is no longer considered magickal.

This is how magick works. There are certain laws that govern how magick works, some of them scientific and some not. These laws are not laws in a sense of a code of conduct that must be follows by all, but rather a statement of the way things are, for example, the law of gravity is not a code of conduct, but rather a statement to explain how certain objects interact.

Magick also has a strong emotional component to it. Emotion drives art, without emotion, art would be lifeless and meaningless. If used properly, emotion can be conveyed through the art making the audience feel what the artist was feeling. Art is the vehicle that allows the person to express their emotions. This is the same in magick. Emotion fuels the energy that we use when performing magick and also allows out intent to be formed. Magick is both an outlet for our emotion but also the vehicle for change. Without the emotion, the intent would not be there, and neither would the energy.

Any emotion can be used to perform magick, as long as it is strong enough. A deep sadness, an overwhelming joy, a raging anger or a profound love work just as well for any kind of working. A word of caution though, the emotion may program the intent, and add fuel, but it should not direct your actions. The decision on what to do, and how to do it should be based on rational thought.

The art of magick applies to the actual techniques and materials used to create the working. In art, one needs to understand your materials and tools and how to use them before you can create art. If you don't know what type of paint, or brushes to use to get the desired effect, your attempts at creating a painting that accurately shows how you feel will be fruitless. The same applies to any form of art, you must know how to use what you want to use before you can use it. A great composer must know how to write music or play an instrument so that the art they create can be recorded. And in the same sense as art, you need to work through various materials, and types of art before you can chose something that works for you.

SYMPATHETIC MAGIC

"If we analyse the principles of thought on which magic is based, they will probably be found to resolve themselves into two: first, that like produces like, or that an effect resembles its cause; and, second, that things which have once been in contact with each other continue to act on each other at a distance after the physical contact has been severed. The former principle may be called the Law of Similarity, the latter the Law of Contact or Contagion." (Frazer, 1922)

Although Frazer had his misgivings about the role of myth and magic for humanity, his writings are some of the most accurate recordings of how magick was practiced and the principles behind why magick works. It is however ironic that most neo-pagans use his work as one of the foremost authorities on paganism, magick and ancient practices.

LAW OF SIMILARITY

In The Golden Bough, Frazer describes the law of Similarity as *"like produces like, or that an effect resembles its cause"* (Frazer, 1922)

This means that if you use an object to represent something, and then cause a change to that object, the change will also be effected on the thing that it represents. For example, a common spell used is to write down a problem of a piece of paper, then charge this piece of paper to represent the problem and then burn or destroy the piece of paper. It is thought that doing this will also destroy the problem itself. Thus the change you effect on the piece of paper, because you have charged it, will be effected on the thing that it represents.

This kind of magick is called Homoeopathic or Imitative Magick.

LAW OF CONTACT OR CONTAGION

In The Golden Bough, Frazer describes the law of Contact or Contagion as *"... things which have once been in contact with each other continue to act on each other at a distance after the physical contact has been severed"* (Frazer, 1922)

This means that if you use a personal object of someone, that object will still have a link to that person, and thus what you do to the object will happen to the person. For example, you can use an article of clothing of a friend to heal that person. The article of clothing enables you to establish a link to that person through it, and thus what happens to the article happens to the person. This is basis used for spells that involve using a person's hair or their nail clippings etc. It is important to remember that the article must just have come in contact with the person, and does not need to be from their body.

This kind of magick is called Contagious Magick.

NEWTON'S LAWS OF MOTION

I appreciate that there are many scientific people out there who would decry the use of Newton's laws to explain magick. I have used these because they are simple for the reader to understand and analogous to many areas of life.

LAW OF INERTIA

"Law I: Every body persists in its state of being at rest or of moving uniformly straight forward, except insofar as it is compelled to change its state by force impressed." – (Newton, 1846)

The Law of Inertia states that things keep going the way they are until something changes them. This law is based on Newton's first law of motion; all I have done is chosen to expand on it, to not only include motion, but also other aspects of life.

In physics this can be explained as a ball that is lying on the ground is at rest, and it will stay at rest (balanced) until an unbalanced force acts upon it. Theoretically, this means that if the wind blows on it from all directions at once, with the same force, the ball will remain still, because the force of the blowing wind is balanced. However, if the wind blowing from one direction is greater or less than the other winds acting upon the ball (unbalanced), the ball will start moving. In the same sense, if a ball is rolling at a constant speed of 10m/s (assume there is no resistance), it will continue rolling at this speed until an unbalanced force acts upon it, and for example the wind blows in the opposite direction.

In magick this means that things will continue the way that they currently are until something happens to change them. If you are in a situation where you hate your job, you will continue to hate your job forever until something happens to change that, either you get fired (and then don't have the job to hate it) or you do something about it, for example speak to your boss and find a resolution.

LAW OF PROPORTION

"Law II: The alteration of motion is ever proportional to the motive force impress'd; and is made in the direction of the right line in which that force is impress'd" (Newton, 1846)

The law of proportion is similar to Newton's second law of motion. Newton's second law of motion states that the change that occurs in things is in proportion to the force of that which changes them.

In physics this can be explained as the amount that an object at rest or moving at a constant speed, changes speed is inversely proportional to the object's mass and directly proportional to the net force of the change and the change will be in the same direction as the net force. If a ball is rolling and a wind blows on it from the opposite direction, the deceleration (negative acceleration) will be directly proportional to the wind speed, and inversely the proportional to the mass of the ball. The heavier the ball (higher the mass), the less the acceleration will be.

In practice this means that the greater the force that imposes on changing an existing situation, the greater the change will be. For example, if you hate your job, and you decide to resign, the change will be drastic, either for the better, or for the worse. However, if you just spoke to your boss honestly about the fact that you don't enjoy your job anymore, the result will less drastic. This is an important law when doing magick, the more energy you use in a spell, the greater the effect of the spell, but remember you may not know all the factors involved, and the effect may not be what you want.

LAW OF RETURN

"Law III: To every action there is always opposed an equal reaction: or the mutual actions of two bodies upon each other are always equal, and directed to contrary parts" (Newton, 1846)

Newton's third law of motion says that for every action, there is an equal and opposite reaction. In physics this can be explained, as the force that you use to push against a wall is equal to the force that the wall is pushing against you.

In magick this means that whatever you do to someone or something else will come back to you equally. I often call this instant Karma. For example, if you kick the dog because you had a bad day at work and the dog bites you, that is an equal (kick = bite) and opposite (you kicked the dog, the dog bit you) reaction. This law ties into the ethics of magick.

THE HERMETIC PRINCIPLES

In the Hermetic teachings there is an acknowledgement that gender is a different thing to sex. Now while this seems unremarkable now, it is important to just give a bit of background into what the Hermetic teachings actually were.

The Hermetic teachings are based on the writings of an author who is referred to as Hermes Trismegistus, or Thoth Hermes Trismegistus who was around in 250 – 300 BCE . He was the first great Egyptian philosopher (Sisowath, 2015) and his writings were so respected that he was said to be in direct communication with the gods, which later lead to him becoming seen as a deity himself. The writings of Thoth Hermes Trismegistus re-emerged in the fifteenth century, although the actual author of these works is unknown and is attributed to the Hermes himself (Hoeller, 1996). The Hermetic teachings are what forms the basis of the Hermetic Order of the Golden Dawn (also referred to as the Golden Dawn) in 1888. The Golden Dawn had many members and links to people who were influential in the founding of modern paganism, namely Aleister Crowley, Dion Fortune, Israel Regardie and A. E. Waite (Cranmer, 1999). Gerald Garner, the father of modern Wicca based many of the teachings on writings by Aleister Crowley (and even that Crowley wrote some of the content himself) (Dearnaley, 2002).

One of the texts that emerged was The Kybalion: Hermetic Philosophy, which was published under the pseudonym of The Three Initiates in 1912 which contains the seven principles, many of which are still used in pagan teachings.

PRINCIPLE OF MENTALISM

"The All is mind; The Universe is Mental." (Three Initiates, 1912)
The principle of mentalism starts with the foundation that the universe (The All) is mind and that all things (be they material, phenomena, matter or energy) are actually all the same and forms part of the universe. It also states that the universe is also simply a manifestation of the all.

To explain this simpler, it is the principle that the universe is everything and everything is also within the universe. For queers we can then extrapolate that to mean that everything in the universe is deserving of the same respect that we would like to receive ourselves.

PRINCIPLE OF CORRESPONDENCE

"*As above, so below; as below so above.*" (Three Initiates, 1912)

The principle of correspondence states that everything that is unknowable is reflected in what we know, everything that is in the spiritual plane is also reflected as phenomena on the material plane.

This principle forms the basis of magick, in that what we create on the material plane (for example a spell or working) is then carried forth onto the spiritual plane where the results become manifested. For queers, the principle of correspondence also allows us to acknowledge that there is nothing about us that is inherently wrong or unnatural. We are manifestations of the divine and the divine is reflective of who we are.

PRINCIPLE OF VIBRATION

"*Nothing rests; everything moves; everything vibrates.*" (Three Initiates, 1912)

The principle of vibration states that everything vibrates, the only difference between matter, energy, mind and spirit is the rate at which it vibrates. There are also varying degrees of vibration, from solid matter which vibrates so slowly that we perceive it to be at rest up to spiritual vibration which is so fast and intense that it cannot be perceived. In magick the principle of vibration allows us to associate specific colours, crystals, herbs and other physical objects with spiritual and mental outcomes.

PRINCIPLE OF POLARITY

"*Everything is Dual; everything has poles; everything has its pair of opposites; like and unlike are the same; opposites are identical in nature, but different in degree; extremes meet; all truths are but half-truths; all paradoxes may be reconciled.*" (Three Initiates, 1912)

The principle of polarity states that everything has polar opposites but that these opposites are what makes the whole. The polar opposites are in fact different aspects of the same thing and that the absolutes don't exist. For example heat and cold are seen as opposites but they are entirely relative to each other, it goes further than saying that without the one the other doesn't exist, it extends to saying that without both neither would exist. It also holds that these polar opposites are just vibrations and that the vibrations can change. The Kybalion also cites the example of love and hate where there can be a sudden and involuntary change from love to hate in our personal lives, so too can there be a change from hate to love.

For queers this can be used to explain our current understanding of gender, it's not that there are two fixed finite concepts that are polar opposites (male and female) but rather that there are varying degrees and subtleties that us all to have varying degrees of both at the same time and the degrees of either can change rapidly or slowly at will.

PRINCIPLE OF RHYTHM

"Everything flows, out and in; everything has its tides; all things rise and fall; the pendulum-swing manifests in everything; the measure of the swing to the right is the measure of the swing to the left; rhythm compensates." (Three Initiates, 1912)

Because of the principle of polarity (described above) there is the principle of rhythm, these polar opposites in everything cause there to be movement. Like an ebb and flow of the sea, the constant movement of the planets around the sun, the movement of the sun in the galaxy and so on. This movement is also manifest in the mind states of people, but the objective is to learn to not be caught in the movement, but rather to control it. For queers, an example of this is stepping out of the gender binary. Rather than be influenced by the societal pressures about what a gender is about, it allows us to step outside of this and choose for ourselves what we want to be. You don't have to wear a dress if you are a girl in the same way that you don't have to be a girl to wear a dress. Studying the principle of rhythm allows us to make conscious choices about which directions we allow ourselves to be pulled in.

PRINCIPLE OF CAUSE AND EFFECT

"Every Cause has its Effect; every Effect has its Cause; everything happens according to Law; Chance is but a name for Law not recognized; there are many planes of causation, but nothing escapes the Law." (Three Initiates, 1912)

The principle of cause and effect is similar to the section on Newton's Laws of Motion (section 1.10) in that every cause has an effect, but also extends out to say that every effect also has a cause. This means that everything that is happening now has a cause, nothing is coincidence. The key is to learn to be a cause, not an effect. We should learn to take control of situations rather than let us carry ourselves along. For queers this can be learning to be a survivor, rather than a victim. It's about taking back your agency and not allowing the events of your past control what will happen in your future.

PRINCIPLE OF GENDER

"Gender is in everything; everything has its Masculine and Feminine Principles Gender; manifests on all planes." (Three Initiates, 1912)

The principle of gender was what intrigued me about the principles and one of the key reasons for it being included in the book. The first thing the principle does is establish that there is a gender, which is separate from physical sex. The next thing the principle establishes is that everything on all planes has both masculine and feminine gender; this means that all matter, energy and people have both a masculine and feminine gender. Note that this is different to saying that all things are either masculine or feminine, but actually that all things are both masculine and feminine. This is what allows us to create, to generate and do magick. For queers the principle of gender confirms that the traditional binary worldview just doesn't apply.

5. ETHICS

There are no commandments for a pagan to follow; the pagan morals and ethics are bound up with the personal ethics of the person. There are however presiding guidelines followed by many pagans, especially Wiccans. These are:

1. *"Eight words the Wiccan Rede fulfil, an' it harm none, do what ye will"* – Doreen Valiente (Holzer, 1971)
2. *"Do what thou wilt shall be the whole of the Law. Love is the law, love under will"* - Aleister Crowley (Crowley, The Book of the Law, 1938)

CONSENT

In magick, as in everyday life it is very important to consider consent when doing any magick for anyone else. Any magick you do is based on your own beliefs, practices and knowledge. Each person, if they are a witch or not, has the ability and the right to make their own decisions and live their own lives; whether we agree with their decisions and beliefs or not.

Doing magick to help someone without their consent means that you could be affecting change in ways that they may not want. There are also times when people's paths need to take them through a really difficult time for them to be able to learn, getting them out of that situation robs them of the opportunity for growth. It's also dangerous because you are taking the control of the situation away from the person, there may be circumstances in the situation that you are not aware of which would change the way you view it.

Magick should always be done with intent for good; but equally it needs to be a measured, carefully considered approach. Sometimes, even if someone does give you consent to do work for them, you need to carefully consider whether you really should do work for them.

THE LAWS OF RETURN

There are various laws that are prescribed amongst some pagans about what happens when you do magick to harm others. These are:
1. The threefold law of return
2. The sevenfold law of return
3. The law of Causality

At the very least you will get back, what you give out. With the threefold and sevenfold laws, you will get back what you gave out multiplied by three or seven respectively.

This of course means that if you do bad things to others, you will get bad things back, and if you do good things to others, good things will return.

Section 3:
Pagan Life

6. LIVING PAGAN

Religion, in many of its forms allows people to understand the world and gives a way for them to interpret the events that unfold around them. They search for the reasons why good things happen and also for ways to prevent or stop bad things from happening. We need a way to control the universe, whether that be by handing it over to a greater power or by beseeching that power to assist them in times of hardship. For me, paganism allows me to take an active part in that cycle. By observing the cycles of the year I have a way to learn about the cycles of nature and take part in them, by doing magick I can make active decisions about what I want. I am able to participate fully in my life and create the destiny of my own choosing.

Living as a pagan means taking responsibility. I am no longer bound to do good things because I was raised a certain way, or because there is a promise of heaven (or hell). I am able to take responsibility for who I am and make active decisions about how I want to live my life. While the past can influence me, I am in charge of making those decisions. I can accept the influence that the past has or I can reject it. For example being pagan has greatly changed the way I interact with people. As a pagan, I do good things because it makes me feel good. Not because I expect anything from the other person, and also not because I believe there are benefits for my soul in the afterlife. I live the way that I want to, and that means being as wonderful as I can to those around me. This doesn't mean that I allow myself to get taken advantage of, far from it.

It does also mean that I get to let myself of the hook when things don't go well. As with many people, I can be quick to anger, especially when I'm feeling frustrated or out of control. The key for me is to be able to understand the thoughts and manage my future actions. If I do get angry, I work at trying to understand the cause. What is it within me that caused me to react in that way to that situation, and once I understand that I can work on the underlying issues that caused the reaction. That doesn't mean I won't get angry again, it just means that I can more easily control the actions associated with the anger. The same can apply to any negative emotions; it's perfectly healthy to experience the full range of emotions, not just the positive ones. We should have moments of great joy alongside the moments of deep despair. The key is being able to control the actions and behaviours associated with these emotions to make sure we aren't doing ourselves or others harm.

BALANCE

Balance is something that the world is obsessed with striving for and ironically, it is the one state of being that can seldom be reached, with perfect balance there would be no movement. Think of an old set of scales, as you add a little to one side, the other side rises, so you add a little to the lighter side and the other side rises. The closest and healthiest way to achieve a kind of balance is not when the disparities between the sides are smallest; it is actually the resilience to be able to right the scales without getting stuck on one side. In practical terms, it doesn't mean never getting angry, just allowing the anger to burn out and see things calmly again without it disrupting your wellbeing. The opposite of this would be hold a grudge, become resentful and to allow the anger to eat you up from the inside.

Balance is also important in terms of our outer lives; we need to find balance between our spiritual, emotional and material sides. We need to find a way to ensure that all parts of ourselves are looked after. Obviously this is impossible to satisfy all at the same time. As you satisfy the emotional (with a relationship or friends), the spiritual and material parts are left behind, so you may get a yearning for your spiritual aspect, thus you fulfil that and the other get left behind. The importance of balance is often overlooked.

I believe that the purpose of being in this form in this incarnation is to learn about balance, when we are in spiritual form we are a completely spiritual being, and we exist for spiritual purposes only. When we are in this incarnation, we are self-aware and sentient and in my opinion, the purpose of being aware of a higher power means that we need to balance between the physical, the emotional, the material and spiritual realms. This does not means that we give up spirituality for a physical world, any less than it means we must give up the material world for spiritualism. The importance is therefore to balance the aspects.

CALLING YOURSELF A WITCH

A witch is anyone who self-identifies as a witch. There are some who believe that you need to have practices paganism, or Wicca, or witchcraft for a certain amount or to a certain level before you can call yourself a witch. There are others who say that being a witch is hereditary, and unless you can prove a pure bloodline you cannot use the term. There are others who say that only women can be witches, and still others who say that only cis women can be witches. Being a witch is a personal choice, you can call yourself a witch if that's what you feel you are. Paganism is about a personal ethos, a relationship with yourself and the world around you. No one else gets to decide for you.

In the same way, you don't have to identify as a witch. You could describe yourself as a pagan, or not disclose to anyone what your beliefs are. It's all a matter of personal choice.

You cannot talk about the term witch without understanding that there is some weight associated to it. For centuries women have been persecuted as witches, this was especially due to Christianity, but is also common in other religions. From the 15th century there was great panic and fear of witches, Europe held witch trails where tens of thousands of women (and men in some areas) were hanged or burned at the stake (bear in mind that they would have been alive when they were set alight). These witch trials later spread to the United States with the most famous being the Salem Witch trials held in 1692. While in developed countries (such as the UK and the United States) the persecution of witches is no longer actively practiced (with the exception of isolated cases) it is important to realise that not all people are as privileged. In many developing countries, such as India and South Africa it may be dangerous for people to be identified as witches (whether they are in fact pagan or not). There are examples of people being killed because they are accused of witchcraft, a shocking example is the Indian authorities have documented that 2097 murders were committed between 2000 and 2012 where witch hunting was the motive (Kapoor, 2015). Compare that to the estimates across the British Isles was around 2000 people executed as witches for the period of 1400CE – 1700CE (Hodgman, 2010). In other countries, such as Saudi Arabia and Central

African Republic, witchcraft (also referred to as sorcery) is actually illegal (Jacobs, 2013).

This all leads me back to my point that the associations the term witch are varied and complicated and self-identifying as a witch is a personal choice, based largely on your own personal circumstances and as such, if someone chooses not to use the term witch, the reasons may be more complicated that you may have initially assumed.

YOUR RELATIONSHIP WITH THE DIVINE

Because of the complications I had with the binary nature of pagan divinity, I spent years not working with any particular deity. I would use generic god and goddess statues without any real emotional connection to them. While this caused me no harm, I do now realise that I was missing out. It was only once I found the deity that I felt attuned to that I actually realised what my previous teachers had been trying to convey.

Attuning to a specific deity brings a great comfort. It's a bit like finding someone who can be both a parent who offers guidance, a friend that shares your thoughts and a sibling who knows you better than you know yourself; all of this without the complicated nature of relationships with other people. The deity you chose to work with can be whoever you chose that fits you best, and finding your deity will actually be a journey as personal to you as your relationship with your deity is.

The most important thing about finding the deity you want to work with is to do research. This can be reading up on anthropological accounts of mythologies, looking at how images of different deities are presented or talking to people about what deities they prefer. The other way to find a deity is through pathworking, meditations or dreams.

Once you have an idea of the deity in question, research them. Get to know their stories, like you would another person, read about them and find out what it is about them that particularly attracts you.

CHOOSING A MAGICKAL NAME

In the queer community especially, a name is more than just a word that everyone calls you by. It can be loaded with meaning depending on where it came from, if it was the name you were given at birth and whether you truly feel it represents you. Because of this, a magickal name is even more important to pagan queers. Your magickal name should be based on your gender and your experience of it.

A magickal name is the name you use when communing with deity, in some traditions it is given to you by your teacher and in others it is chosen by the initiate themselves while on a pathworking. A magickal name is also associated with starting out a new path; it can be used as a new name to represent the new identity that you are forging. Your magickal name does not need to be set for life, as you evolve and grow you can change it.

Your magickal name should reflect an aspect of who you are or who you are becoming. It can be based on a deity, plant, herb, crystal or element until you are more comfortable with what magickal path that you want to follow. You can also choose a name made of various things, for example Lone Wolf.

Your magickal name may also be secret if you choose it to be. In some traditions it is believed that your magickal name can be used to bind you, and to prevent this people have a coven name (which they use to protect their non magickal mundane identity) and a magickal name that they use when communing with deity. You may choose to keep to this tradition if it suits you.

ETHICS OF LOVE SPELLS

The most common use for magick in mass media is love spells, and who doesn't identify with the idea of being alone and getting someone to fall madly in love with you, just at the flick or a wand or the swallowing of a potion? In the queer world relationships can be even more complicated; after all, most people just want to be loved. Where's the harm in that?

This is of course the big question. The problem with the idea of love spells is that they are usually aimed at a specific person. It is often based on the idea that one person is in love with someone else (who for the purposes of clarity we'll call the castee) but that love is not reciprocated. Leaving all doubts about the ability of magick to control or create a situation aside, this is where the trouble starts. The castee no longer has agency in the situation, they don't have any free will because they are being magically manipulated into loving the other person. This is the basis for abuse. In all relationships the foundation should be mutual trust, the castee cannot trust the person who started it all and is vulnerable because no matter how bad the behaviour of the person, the castee is magickally compelled to remain in the relationship.

This of course has an unintended consequence, if you could get someone to magickally fall in love with you, the relationship is about control, not about mutual respect and thus will ultimately unfulfilling. What we get from relationships (romantic and otherwise) is connection, the sense that you are valued for who you are and that the other person cares about you in spite of (or because of) what you perceive as your faults. If you have forced them into loving you, you don't get that. You'll never trust that the person really does love you or if it is the effect of the spell you cast.

This isn't completely hopeless though, lonely queers are not doomed to be alone because of their ethics, quite the opposite actually. There are ways that you can cast spells ethically and still be able to get what you truly desire, it just might not be what you expect.

7. THE SABBATS

The eight festivals in a pagan year represent the four seasons' start and mid-points, and are approximately six weeks apart and are known as Sabbats. Not all eight are celebrated by all pagans, some pagans only celebrate half, one or even none of the festivals through the year. The celebration of the festival can be a ritual, a gathering or just a personal remembrance of the day.

Considering that the Sun represents the God, and the moon the Goddess it makes sense that some pagans follow the wheel of the year by the activities of the cycle of birth and rebirth of the God during those times. For example, at Yule, the winter solstice, it is believed that the Sun God is reborn and he matures throughout the year to his peak at Litha, the summer solstice, where he is at his strongest. After Litha he weakens through the year until his death at Samhain. The source of this mythology can be seen as a more 'primitive' people needing to understand how the cycles of the year work. It can also be seen as coincidental that the celebrations occur when the community would get together to celebrate the seasons, and thus folk tales became legend and legend became deity.

The celebration of the wheel of the year is the recognition of the cyclical nature of life, starting with birth, life, death and then rebirth. It is also seen as a good way to attune with nature and understand the natural world around you. When doing your Sabbat celebration, try to follow what works for you. If the a book says that at Lammas you must have sunflowers on your altar, find out what flowers at that time in your area, and make that work for you. Figure out what fruits or vegetables are available at that specific time of year and use those in your rituals. These are just a few ways of making the Sabbats real for you and attuning with the world around you.

The southern hemisphere celebrates the Sabbats are the opposite time to the northern hemisphere because we are on the opposite end of the equator and our seasons are opposite. So Beltane would be celebrated on the 1st of May in Europe and the US, in South Africa and Australia it would be celebrating Samhain. Keeping in tune with the seasons for your hemisphere makes sense, it just wouldn't make sense to dance around a maypole and celebrate fertility at the beginning of winter.

YULE

Season Point: Midwinter – Winter Solstice
Approximate date: 21/22 December – Northern Hemisphere (21/22 June - Southern Hemisphere)

Yule is the midwinter festival, celebrated at the winter solstice. The winter solstice is the time of year when the sun is farthest from us and we therefore have the shortest day and the longest night. Yule celebrations are often carried out through the night and the celebrants then stay awake to watch the sun rise.

According to myth, Yule is the time of year when the God is borne from the Goddess. Yule is the celebration of the return of the God, and therefore the return of the sun, warmth and light. This is why the celebrations usually carry on until dawn, because dawn represents the official birth of the God from the Goddess.

Celebrations of Yule are remarkably similar to those of include Christmas and include a Yule tree (usually a pine) and evergreen plants to represent the return of life to the world. Depending on the tradition, the celebrants may decorate the tree with candles, lights and decorations. In most traditions, small handmade gifts are exchanged. Another tradition is to light a Yule log, and keep it burning throughout the night or for at least twelve hours, to bring beneficial magick, for example good crops, blessings on the house and protection. A yule log that is more practical is to make a Yule log (the cake kind), cover it with melted chocolate and sprinkle with icing sugar. Place one candle on the Yule log for each of the celebrants (birthday candles work the best for this). Each celebrant then lights the candle as they make a wish. Once everyone has made a wish, the celebrants blow out the candles and eat the Yule log.

Yule is a time of renewal, the beginning of new things and the return of life. It is a time of great celebration and feasting. Now is the time to start new ventures, especially ones that will last throughout the year or longer.

IMBOLC

Season Point: Start of Spring
Approximate date: 1 February – Northern Hemisphere (1 August - Southern Hemisphere)

Imbolc is celebrated at the midpoint between the winter solstice and vernal/ spring equinox. It is the time of year that the first blooms start appearing for the start of spring.

According to myth it is the time of that the goddess has started puberty, and the potential of her being fertile is realised.

It is said that on Imbolc, the Goddess Brighid walks on the earth, and to celebrate Imbolc, before going to bed, the ashes are swept from the fire pit, and strips of cloth placed on the windowsill for the Goddess Brighid to bless. In the morning, the people would look in the ashes for evidence of the goddess's passing. The cloth strips are said to have powers of protection and healing.

Imbolc is a time of the hopes of Yule start coming to fruition. Imbolc is also a time to start planting things that will grow into fruition during Beltane and Litha, the harvest festivals.

OSTARA

Season Point: Mid-spring – Vernal/ Spring equinox
Approximate date: 20/21 March - Northern Hemisphere (21/22 September – Southern Hemisphere)

Ostara is held at the Vernal/ Spring equinox, this is when the day and night are of the same length and the days start becoming longer. This is a time of year known for its fertility and growth.

Ostara is characterized by the re-joining of the Mother Goddess and her lover-consort-son, who spent the winter months in death. Other variations include the young God regaining strength in his youth after being born at Yule, and the Goddess returning to her Maiden aspect.

Because of the association of fertility and growth, celebrations of Ostara include painting eggs with your hopes for the coming year and then burying them. On the morning of Ostara, it is tradition to search for the eggs, and if they have been uncovered the Goddess will grant those wishes in the year to come. This time of year is also associated with rabbits and hares.

Ostara is a celebration of the return of spring and growth, the renewal of life that appears on the earth after the winter. It is a time to start new projects and celebrate the coming of summer.

BELTANE

Season Point: Start Summer
Approximate date: 1 May - Northern Hemisphere (1 November - Southern Hemisphere)

Beltane is held halfway between the spring/vernal equinox and the summer solstice and is the official start of summer. It marks the time of year when fertility rites are performed and the earth is celebrated.

In lore, this is the time of year when the Goddess and the God consummate their relationship which is celebrated with a dance around the maypole (seen to represent that God's phallus being covered by the Goddess).

Beltane is a time of celebration and fertility; it is often celebrated by young lovers as a time for sex, fun and frolicking. It's the time of year for spells of growth and bounty and handfastings that take place on Beltane are said to be fruitful and long lasting.

LITHA

Season Point: Midsummer – Summer Solstice
Approximate date: 20/21 June - Northern Hemisphere (21/22 December-Southern Hemisphere)

On this day, the noon of the year, light and life are abundant. This is the longest day of the year, the Summer Solstice, when the sun is at its highest and the start of winter will soon begin.

It is a time of promise; it is not yet a time of the harvest. The lambs have been born but are not ready for slaughter and while the crops are growing tall, they are not ready to be harvested yet. It is a time of year where there is still a risk that that the land will not be fruitful.

This is the time of year when the God is at his strongest and the Goddess is pregnant in time for the birth at

Contrasted with Yule when we look inward in meditative silence, Midsummer sets us to a time when our focus is turned outward, joyfully experiencing the delights of the Lord and Lady's abundance. We delight in the first fruits of the season and revel in the company of others, dancing with wild abandon in a blissful celebration of the season.

LAMMAS/LUGHNASADH

Season Point: Start Autumn
Approximate date: 1 August – Northern Hemisphere (1 February – Southern Hemisphere)

Lammas, also known as Lughnasadh, is celebrated at the midpoint between the summer solstice and the autumnal equinox. It's a time when the harvests of corn and wheat are gathered.

In myth the God starts to grow weaker as the Goddess's belly grows fuller, she is sad for the loss of the God but is hopeful because he will be reborn through her.

Lammas is the celebration of the first harvest and is celebrated with bread, loaves and an abundance of crops. It is a time of great feasting, thankfulness and appreciation. This is the time of year where the plans made at Imbolc and planted in Ostara come to fruition.

MABON

Season Point: Mid-Autumn – Autumnal Equinox
Approximate date: 21/22 September – Northern Hemisphere (20/21 March – Southern Hemisphere)

Mabon is held at the Autumnal equinox and is the point at which the days begin to get shorter and the nights longer. The chill of the weather is starting to be felt.

In lore, the God prepares for his death at Mabon. This makes Mabon a more sombre celebration in comparison to Lammas/Lughnasadh as we are both giving thanks for the bounty but also preparing for the winter ahead.

Mabon is the second harvest and is the time of year where the farm animals are slaughtered if there is not enough feed for them to be kept over winter.

SAMHAIN

Season Point: Start of Winter
Approximate date: 31st October – Northern Hemisphere (1 May - Southern Hemisphere)

Samhain is the start of winter, and is a time for pagans to remember those that have passed both in the preceding year and the time before. This is sometimes a time of solemn ritual, but it can also be a celebration of the lives that have touched us and passed on.

In Myth, this is the time of year that the god has died at Mabon, and the Goddess in her mourning prepares for the God's rebirth at Yule thus beginning the cycle of the year again.

The night before Samhain is known as 'All Hallows eve' and this has then transferred into the Halloween festivals popularised in 20th century culture. To celebrate Samhain, one can light candles to remember, and when doing the libation (cakes and ale), you can offer the libation to those departed.

8. THE ESBATS

The moon is representative of the Goddess, thus spells and workings done under the moon are affected by it. Remember, the moon affects everything, whether done in day or night. It may be a good idea to attune yourself to the moon and bear in mind the moon's influence when making even mundane decisions. A ritual done to celebrate the phases of the moon is called an esbat, so you can have a full moon esbat (to celebrate the full moon or a dark moon esbat to celebrate the dark moon).

Each full moon cycle is named based on where in the year it falls, and these can also vary based on the hemisphere and local area. Technically a Blue Moon is when there are 4 moons in a season (instead of the normal 3) the third moon in that season is called a blue moon. The easier way to work it out is that the second moon in a calendar month is the Blue Moon (thus the saying 'once in a Blue Moon' actually literally refers to once a year). The following moon names are based on the English Moon names and are split by season:
- Winter Moons:
    - December – Moon Before Yule
    - January - Moon After Yule
    - February - Wolf Moon
- Spring Moons:
    - March - Lenten Moon
    - April – Egg Moon,
    - May – Milk Moon
- Summer Moons:
    - June – Flower Moon

- July - Hay Moon
- August – Grain Moon
- Autumn Moons:
    - September - Fruit Moon
    - October – Harvest Moon
    - November – Hunter's Moon

If you apply the same moon names to the Southern Hemisphere, it is split as follows:

- Winter Moons:
    - June – Moon Before Yule
    - July - Moon After Yule
    - August - Wolf Moon
- Spring Moons:
    - September - Lenten Moon
    - October – Egg Moon,
    - November – Milk Moon
- Summer Moons:
    - December – Flower Moon
    - January - Hay Moon
    - February – Grain Moon
- Autumn Moons:
    - March - Fruit Moon
    - April – Harvest Moon
    - May – Hunter's Moon

DARK MOON

This is the time when the moon is not visible from the earth, it a time of breaking off old and starting anew. This is a good time for getting rid of old habits. This is also known as a New moon.

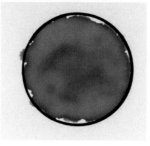

WAXING MOON

This is from dark moon to full moon; the moon is getting fuller and becoming more and more visible daily. This is a good time for anything that involves growing, getting bigger, more, fertility etc. For example, starting a new job, or planting herbs in the garden, trying to fall pregnant

FULL MOON

This is the time when the moon is most visible to us. This is a good time for fertility, but less steady growth than the Waxing moon. The Full moon is more about a once-off gain.

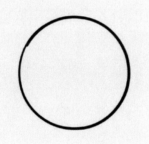

WANING MOON

This is when the moon is slowly becoming less and less visible to us. This is a time for slowly letting go of bad things, and things drawing to a close.

Section 4:
Meditation Practices

9. VISUALISATION, MEDITATION AND PATHWORKING EXERCISES

Meditation is introspective, visualisation is focusing on something outside of you and pathworking is travelling on a specific path to a goal. All of these take practice and focus to be able to do. None of these are completely outside of the ability for anyone.

MEDITATION

The key to meditation is the ability to just be with yourself. Your focus should be on your body, not on your surroundings. Although it is difficult to still our minds there are a number of ways to overcome these interruptions, and with practice the interruptions may still come, but they will be easier to ignore. There are various schools of thought and different methods to use when meditating, it is important that you use the method which feels right to you. It may be that your own intuition will lead you to select a method of your own and, if that is the case, then that technique is the one you should use. Try to meditate daily, either first thing in the morning or just before you go to bed. Start small, just two minutes a day is a very good start, once you are comfortable with two minutes you can start to increase the amount of time you meditate for. It's also useful to meditate before you start a ritual or spell to make sure that you are in the right headspace before beginning. Keep a meditation journal, and jot down a few words to describe how you felt about the meditation and if you received any important insights. It's also important to note the days when it's been difficult or challenging so you can look back on it later to see how far you've come, or understand what struggles you still need to overcome.

With most meditation practices start off finding a comfortable position, sitting on a chair, sitting on a mat or lying down. Focus on slowing your breathing, taking deep in breaths, holding for a few seconds and then exhaling. Do not overexert yourself or hold your breath longer than is comfortable. The importance is in slowing the breath and taking deep breathes into your chest.

BREATHING MEDITATION

Close your eyes. Breathe in slowly, filling your lungs with air, and then release the breath again. Try to achieve a slow regular rhythm of breathing - it is often helpful to count to three while breathing in and then again while breathing out. Eventually you will reach a stage where the counting is no longer necessary and where you are able to maintain that slow even rhythm naturally and without difficulty. The advantage of this particular technique is that, if you are really concentrating upon your breathing process, it is impossible for your mind to be distracted by all the trivial thoughts which may try to present themselves. You may well find that when you first begin to meditate by this method, you are unable to sustain it for very long before your mind begins to wander and to become engulfed in day-to-day problems. It is better not to force yourself to continue but to accept the fact that the meditative state does become easier to maintain with practice. If you are able to set aside a particular time each day as well as a particular private place in which to practise your meditation, this too will help you to develop the ability.

MEDITATION USING A CRYSTAL AS A FOCUS

I have found that when mediating it is often useful to have something to meditate on. I usually use a crystal or gemstone to meditate, as this allows me to focus and shut out all other thoughts from my mind. Place the crystal in your receptive hand (the opposite one to the one you write with), Concentrate on the crystal, feel weight in your hand, is it heavy or lighter than you expect it to be based on its size? Feel the way it presses into your hand and the amount of effort it takes to hold it in place. Now spend a few moments concentrating on the shape of it in your hand, feel for the smooth sides, the edges, the roughness and any sharp points. Just concentrate on the physical shape it has. Now try to feel what feelings you have coming from the crystal, does it feel peaceful, forceful, warm, cold. What images come to mind when holding the crystal? Once you have a firm understanding of the crystal, focus again on your breathing, taking deep in and out breaths, feel the breath deep in your chest. Do this for a few moments before opening your eyes.

This meditation technique is used when an initiate is learning to work with crystals, it allows one to connect with the crystal and develop a deeper understanding of what the crystal means. It's recommended to keep a journal or book of shadows nearby so you can write down any thoughts you have from the meditation and also so you can track your progress. It's advisable to take it slowly, meditate on a specific crystal for a few sessions before moving onto the next one. As you practice the meditation and the communication with the crystals becomes simpler.

MEDITATION FOR DYSPHORIA

Many queers experience dysphoria of some sort or another, it can either be about a specific aspect of their body that doesn't fit or general sense of not being comfortable in your own skin. This meditation is aimed at easing some of that and aims to assist you with getting a general sense of the body outside of the dysphoria. This meditation will not cure dysphoria, but is a way to manage the anxiety and stress that can come from these intense feelings of discomfort. It allows you to take some time and just connect with your body; all the different cells and nerve endings that allow you to do all the things that you enjoy doing.

Lie comfortably on the floor, close your eyes and concentrate on your breathing. Do not at this stage aim to control your breathing at all, just focus on the breath going in through the mouth and nose, feel it moving into your chest, feel your chest expand, now breathe out, feeling your chest contract and the air pushing its way out of your nose and mouth. Do this for a few breaths, just concentrating on the sensation of breathing in and out. We're going to focus on each part of the body, concentrating on contracting and relaxing each of the muscle groups in turn. Start at your feet. Focus on contracting the muscles in your toes as you breathe in and release as you breathe out. Next move to your feet, contracting on the in breathe and relaxing on the out breath. Now move up your feet to your ankles, contract on the in breath and relax on the out breath. Next your calves, contract on the in breath, relax on the out breath. Now your knees, contract on the in breath and relax on the out breath. Continue with the contracting and relaxing each of your muscle groups in turn, you don't need to know a detailed physiology, just do what feels natural. Move up your legs, your buttocks, you pelvic area, your stomach, your chest, arms, hands, shoulders, neck, face and finally your head. When you are ready, go back to the deep breathing that we did at the start. Breathe in through your nose and mouth, feel the air pushing into your lungs, rising your chest, expanding your body cavity and breathe out though your nose and mouth. Do this a few times until you feel ready to slowly open your eyes and re-enter the world.

VISUALISATION

Visualisation is the ability to create a picture in your mind, and focus on it. Visualisation is used when doing spells and working or when invoking deity or the elements. Most people can already create mental images, but as the focus on the image, and the daily thoughts start poking through, people find it hard to maintain the image.

PRACTICAL EXERCISE FOR VISUALISATION

I find that the best place to start with visualisations is to use something that is physically there, for example an apple. Place the apple on a table in front of you. Focus on it, look at the shape, the size, the angles of the light, the colour, the smell. Firmly imprint the picture of the apple in your mind. Once you have the picture in your mind, close your eyes. Now keep the image of the apple in your mind. Rotate it, bring it closer, and move it further away. Focus on the apple, and place it back in the original position. Now open your eyes, and see how different the mental image of the apple was from the real apple.

Once you have mastered visualisation, you will be able to create mental images without needing the actual object.

WHITE LIGHT MEDITATION

Once you are comfortable with meditation, you may find it useful to meditate while visualising. This meditation starts with being comfortable, focus on your breathing, close your eyes so that you will not be distracted by external factors. As you breathe slowly and evenly, visualise pure white light entering your mind and your body. With practice you will actually feel the light entering every part of you as you breathe in and then, as you exhale, allow the light to leave you and spread its goodness into the atmosphere around you.

PATHWORKING

A pathworking is guided meditation where, rather than focusing on a specific thing (such as a crystal) the pathworking follows a story that results at a point where a message is received. This is a good technique to use for people who find meditation difficult, but can also be used when trying to discover answers to specific questions. A pathworking is a combination of meditation and astral projection. It is called pathworking because it is explained as exploring the paths on the tree of life.

Pathworkings are usually led by someone who has experience in writing and reading pathworkings and can consist of anything from reading through a ritual (which allows the initiates to complete the ritual on the astral plane rather than in the physical) to a simple story that allows the initiates to wander through a wood and find an answer or meet someone.

Although most commonly led by another, I have found that leading your own pathworking a very effective way of meditating and getting answers. Most often I use a pathworking just before I go to sleep, which means that if I fall asleep during the pathworking I may actually receive the answer while I am dreaming.

The key to self-pathworking is to ensure that you have a plan for the path before you begin. Because of this I use the same pathworking all the time and the results then match to my intent; this means that I can focus on my intent and my outcome rather than thinking ahead to what the next step is.

ASTRAL TEMPLE

The Astral temple is a place that you create for yourself in the spiritual realm where you can work, rest and even play when you are in need of a spiritual place but you do not have a physical space at your disposal. Your astral temple can also be used to perform magick, as what you do in your Astral Temple will affect the physical realm as well. When you travel to your Astral temple, you enter into a deep meditation, a trance like state where you then move into your temple.

Your Astral temple can be a temple to your chosen deity or just to nature in general but it depends on who you are, what makes you comfortable and how you view your spirituality. Don't pay too much attention on what you want your astral temple to be, just focus on going there and see what it is like. Your subconscious will build the Astral temple for you, based on who you are, and what you needs are. My astral temple is usually just a clearing in a forest but your astral temple will suit you, there is no reason why it cannot be aboard a space station or even underwater. They physical limitations of this world do not apply in the astral temple, if everything floats in your astral temple then so be it. It is your space and yours alone.

Get comfortable, relax your body, and go into a meditative state. Imagine your Astral Temple, pay attention to the details, for example, the floor, how does it feel against your feet? What is the temperature of the area? Is it warm or cool? What can you see? What colours are things? How much light is there, is it bright or dim?

The first few times just focus on getting there, and getting to know the place. The more you go there the more solid the astral temple becomes in your mind. Try going to the astral temple every evening, in bed, before going to sleep. The first few times you will fall asleep either before getting there or as you get there, this is normal! Keep going, the more you practice, the better you will get. This is both because you are training your mind to focus on meditation, and because you are getting to know your astral temple piece by piece.

PRACTICAL ENERGY EXERCISE

Place your projective hand (the one you write with), approximately an inch above your partner's receptive hand (the opposite to the one you write with), palms facing. Both people close your eyes and focus on sending energy through your palm onto the palm of the other person. Don't get stuck on how to send the energy, imagine white light, or heat or electricity flowing from your body, down your arm and out through your hand.

The person receiving the energy will not necessarily feel a blinding white light, or an intense heat. More than likely, you will feel a little movement, or a tingling feeling. That is feeling energy. It doesn't have to be a mind blowing, Hollywood-style experience for it to be real. The more you work with energy, the stronger the energy you will send, the easier it will be to send and the more you will feel the distinct feeling of energy.

Once you can work with energy and manipulate the energy, you can do various things, for example spells, workings, healing and rituals.

RAISING ENERGY

Energy is no great mystery but we need to be able to raise energy So we can use it in circles, for spells or in ritual. There are a few ways of raising energy:

- Movement: All forms of movement raise energy; the main fault with this method is the body tends to use up most the energy that has been raised. Types of movement can include, dance, running, jumping, yoga, clenching and unclenching of the muscles in the body, sexual intercourse etc.
- Voice: Chanting, Singing, Dialogue and Vocal Pronunciations all raise energy, because of the close ties with our emotions. You can see the form of raising energy in most religious practices throughout the world.
- Meditation: Using meditation for example working with the chakras or aura, focusing, visualisation can be used to raise energy. It must however be noted that Meditation, in itself has more effective uses than raising energy.
- Focusing: One can focus on a visual point, for example a star, the moon, a candle, a fire etc., to draw the energy towards you.
- Sound: Listening to music can raise your emotions, which in turn can raise energy.
- Movement and sound: This can raise a lot of energy because you are using both the movement to make the sound, and the sound itself for example drumming, clapping, stomping etc.

Depending on what you need, you can use a combination of many of the above ways of raising energy together to create greater amounts of energy; for example, you can sing, dance, focus and clap your hands all at the same time. Many Wiccan covens and other practices, use the above practices to raise energy, which the High Priestess will then focus on the working.

GROUNDING ENERGY

After working with the energy, you need to ground to get rid of any of the excess. This means that you move all excess the energy from within and around you into the earth, hence the name grounding. How do you know you need to ground? You will most likely feel jittery, jumpy and a little off-kilter, very similar to the effects of a sugar high.

There are two main ways to ground energy. Though mediation, where you focus on pulling all the excess energy towards you, and then focus it into a white light that pours the excess energy into the earth for earth healing. The simpler way to ground energy is to eat salty, heavy protein rich and fatty foods. The foods that make you feel full and satisfied. It may also be worth noting that immediately after working with energy you should avoid food or drinks high in sugar or alcohol as both of these may prevent you grounding.

CHAKRAS

The chakras are energy centres along the body. These chakras are the location of life force (prana/ chi/ shakti) and are thought to give life to the physical body and associated with interactions of physical, emotional and mental states. The function of the chakras is to spin and draw in this Universal Life Force Energy to keep the spiritual, mental, emotional and physical health of the body in balance. Depending on the source, some references refer to anywhere between five and eight chakras along the human body.

There are some that believe that the source of all the energy (Kundalini) lies in the base of the spine, and that through meditation and different forms of Yoga, one can evoke this energy and cause it rise through the chakras until it passes through the crown chakra and godhead is touched. There are other schools of thought that believe that by evoking the Kundalini and passing this energy through the crown chakra, one will lose the ability to relate to the outside world.

Links have been made between the position and purpose of the chakras to the positions of the glands in the Endocrine system. Below is a picture showing the positions of the chakras:

THE CROWN CHAKRA (SAHASRARA)

Chakra: The Crown Chakra (Sahasrara)
Colour: White or Violet
Primary Functions: Connection to the Divine
Associated Element: Space/ Thought
Stones that can be used: Clear quartz, amethyst and sugilite.

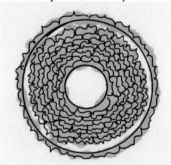

Found at the crown of the head, this chakra is the centre of cosmic energies, universal energies, the life force, spirituality and connection with the godhead. The crown chakra is said to be the chakra of consciousness, the master chakra that controls all the others. Its role would be very similar to that of the pituitary gland, which secretes hormones to control the rest of the endocrine system, and also connects to the central nervous system via the hypothalamus. The thalamus is thought to have a key role in the physical basis of consciousness. Symbolised by a lotus with a thousand petals.

THE THIRD EYE CHAKRA (AJNA)

Chakra: The Third Eye Chakra (Ajna)
Colour: Indigo
Primary Functions: Intuition, Extra-sensory perception, Psychicism
Associated Element: time / light
Stones that can be used: Lapis lazuli, sodalite, fluorite, sugilite, celestite and clear quartz.

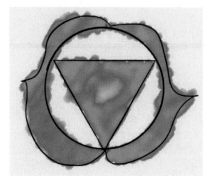

Found between the eyebrows, it is related to the eyes, nose, throat and sinuses and is the centre of intuition, psychic development. **The third eye** is linked to the pineal gland. Ajna is the chakra of time and awareness and of light. The pineal gland is a light sensitive gland that produces the hormone melatonin, which regulates the instincts of going to sleep and awakening. It has been conjectured that it also produces trace amounts of the psychedelic chemical dimethyltryptamine. Symbolised by a lotus with two petals.

THE THROAT CHAKRA (VISHUDDHA)

Chakra: The Throat Chakra (Vishuddha)
Colour: azure, blue
Primary Functions: speech, self-expression, communication
Associated Element: life / sound
Stones that can be used: Blue lace agate, lapis lazuli, turquoise, celestite, fluorite, aquamarine and moonstone.

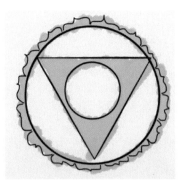

Found in the v of the collarbone, it is the centre of self-expression, communication of any kind and thought. The throat chakra is said to be related to communication and growth, growth being a form of expression. This chakra is paralleled to the thyroid, a gland that is also in the throat, and which produces thyroid hormone, responsible for growth and maturation. Symbolised by a lotus with sixteen petals.

THE HEART CHAKRA (ANAHATA)

Chakra: The Heart Chakra (Anahata)
Colour: green
Primary Functions: devotion, love, compassion, healing
Associated Element: air
Stones that can be used: Green jade, malachite, aventurine, rose quartz and amazonite.

Found at mid breastbone level with the heart, this chakra is the centre for love, compassion for the self and for others. The heart chakra is related to higher emotion, compassion, love, equilibrium, and well-being. It is related to the thymus, located in the chest. This organ is part of the immune system, as well as being part of the endocrine system. It produces T cells responsible for fighting off disease, and is adversely affected by stress.

Symbolised by a lotus with twelve petals.

THE SOLAR PLEXUS CHAKRA (MANIPURA)

Chakra: The Solar Plexus Chakra (Manipura)
Colour: Yellow
Primary Functions: mental functioning, power, control, freedom to be oneself, career
Associated Element: fire
Stones that can be used: Topaz, Citrine and tiger's eye.

Found at the solar plexus, this chakra is the centre for personal power, ego, self-confidence and action. The solar plexus chakra is related to the transition from base to higher emotion, energy, assimilation and digestion, and is said to correspond to the roles played by the pancreas and the outer adrenal glands, the adrenal cortex. These play a valuable role in digestion, the conversion of food matter into energy for the body. Symbolised by a lotus with ten petals.

THE SACRAL CHAKRA (SWADHISTHANA)

Chakra: The Sacral Chakra (Swadhisthana)
Colour: orange
Primary Functions: emotion, sexual energy, creativity
Associated Element: water
Stones that can be used: Carnelian, tiger's eye, bloodstone

Found two inches below the navel, it works with the kidneys, bladder, digestive system and reproductive system. The sacral chakra is located in the groin, and is related to base emotion, sexuality and creativity. This chakra is said to correspond to the testicles or the ovaries, that produce the various sex hormones involved in the reproductive cycle, which can cause dramatic mood swings. Symbolised by a lotus with six petals.

THE BASE CHAKRA (MULADHARA)

Chakra: The Base Chakra (Muladhara)
Colour: red or coral red
Primary Functions: instinct, survival, security
Associated Element: earth
Stones that can be used: Obsidian, hematite, smoky quartz, garnet, ruby, jasper, carnelian, bloodstone.

The base chakra is found at the base of the spine, its colour is red. Works with the spinal column, large intestine and bones. Centre for security and safety, material concerns and wellbeing, this is your foundation. The **base/ root chakra** is related to instinct, security, survival and also to basic human potentiality. This centre is located in the region between the genitals and the anus. Although no endocrine organ is placed here, it is said to relate to the inner adrenal glands, the adrenal medulla, responsible for the fight and flight response when survival is under threat. In this region is located a muscle that controls ejaculation in the sexual act. Symbolised by a lotus with four petals.

Section 5:
Magickal Correspondences

10. MAGICKAL CORRESPONDENCES

Magickal correspondences work on the basis that something provokes an emotion. Therefore by using that thing in a working, that emotion (or properties will also be invoked) and will add to the spell for example, if you are doing a protection spell, you could use sandalwood and perform the spell on a Saturday and in the waxing moon to add to the protection of the spell.

This is used in a sense that for example, the colour Red represents the base charka, and the element of fire, the masculine divine and the emotions such as rage and passion and may other associations. When gazing at the moon, it evokes certain emotions from you and therefore those become the association to use.

You can use the magickal associations in every aspect of life for example when creating a working, a spell, choosing how to decorate your altar or your home, choosing when would be a good time to speak to your boss about a promotion (Wednesday or Sunday) or when to tell someone you love them (Friday).

PANTHEONS

A pantheon is a collection of deities from a specific culture, for example the Greek, Roman or Celtic pantheons. There are many resources available to explore the different Gods and Goddesses from the different pantheons. Spend time going through them, reading their stories and find a deity that works for you. If you find that you cannot find a specific deity that works for you, make one up. Create an image of the deity and what you feel they represent, and use that. You needn't name them, just call upon them. By having a generic deity concept you can change their representations depending on what aspect of them you need.

Do what feels right. If you chose to only work with one deity that, to you, represents both male and female then do so. Remember, magick only works if you feel it, and believe it. If you choose a deity that you don't identify with then chances are, the magick won't work.

NON-BINARY DEITIES

To represent the non-binary deity, I have chosen to combine the symbols for the Goddess and God. The associated colour is bronze or purple.

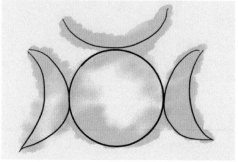

It is difficult to separate the non-binary deity concepts as much of what is written and known about the different gods and goddesses is filtered through the binary worldviews of both historians and academics. The impact of colonialization on the truth of who these deities were and how they were worshipped is cannot be emphasised enough. There are examples of deities who change gender (for example Loki who changed gender to 'trick' unsuspecting humans, or Artemis who by being a huntress is said to be androgynous and thus can be seen to represent the 'masculine' aspects of hunting, determination and honour). There are also more androgynous characters who seem to have no gender. There are a lot of deities that are beyond the standard binary, where there is a range from a wealth of information or very little written about them. I have tried as far as possible to list all the verifiable non-binary deities here, while also being conscious of not appropriating another culture. Once again, before you use any deity, do your research about them and try and be as culturally sensitive as possible.

Examples are Ardhanaishvara (Hindu), Atum (Egyptian), Neith (Egyptian), Hermaphroditu/ Hermaphroditus (Greek), Athena (Greek), Baal (Ancient Palestine), Baphomet (Templars), Amaterasu (Shinto), Toyuke (Shinto), Kayanuhime (Shinto), Dionysus (Greek), Iphis/Iphys (Greek).

THE UNIVERSAL

Before I even considered using a non-binary deity, I used the idea of a Universal. The Universal is the very stuff that the entire universe is made of and is thus entirely beyond gender. It is almost an embodiment of the very matter that we are all made of at a sub-atomic level. I have include the Universal as a deity, not because I believe that there is some super-god above all that rules over the other gods and goddesses, but because it is the worship of all matter and being and the recognition of the interconnectedness of us all.

This concept of a Universal deity that is throughout everything sometimes referred to as Dryghtyn (MacTara, 1999) and is seen to be the universal energy that all the deities spring from. The Universal is not to be worshipped but revered. The Hermetic traditions teach that *"While All is in The All, it is equally true that The All is in All."* (Three Initiates, 1912).

COMMON GODS

Below is a list of the more common Gods and Goddesses used by many modern pagans. A short description is given of each, but make sure that you read up about the deity before you begin working with them, to make sure they fit what you want to do.

The God symbol shows the god with a representation of horns above his head, and is associated with the colour gold.

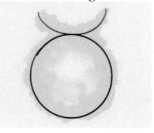

GODS OF THUNDER

Gods of thunder are often portrayed as large, powerful men and are known for their protective patriarchal nature. The god of thunder will often be the leader of the gods, or the head of an army. These Gods are associated with storms, and more specifically thunder. They can be invoked for strength, protection, justice and for courage.

Examples are Thor (Norse), Zeus (Greek), Jupiter (Roman), Taranis (Celtic)

SUN GODS

The Sun Gods are associated with the sky and the sun; they are seen to bring light and warmth and thus growth. They can be invoked for growth, fertility (especially male fertility), fire and healing.

Examples are Freyr (Norse), Helios (Greek), Sol (Roman), Re (Egyptian), Belenus (Celtic), Utu (Sumerian)

THE SEA GODS

The gods of the sea and oceans can also lead them to being associated with storms and destruction. They can be invoked for safe journeys over water, or over long distances and for revenge.

Examples are Aegir/ **Ægir** (Norse), Poseidon (Greek), Neptune (Roman), Manannan (Celtic), Manawydan ap Llyr (Welsh).

THE HUNTER GODS

The hunter gods are often young gods associated with the hunt and are also associated with young men and young warriors. The Hunter Gods can be invoked for passion, courage and to attain a goal successfully.

Examples are Njord (Norse), Orion (Greek), Anhur (Egyptian), Cernunnos (Celtic)

GODS OF KNOWLEDGE & WISDOM

The gods of knowledge and intellect are more nuanced than the more prominent gods in many traditions. For example, they can be associated with assisting to strategize in war and battles, but also for their creation and poetry. These gods are also associated with death and magickal knowledge of immortality.

They can be invoked for finding things out, studying, communing with the dead and for divination.

Examples are Odin (Norse), Enki (Sumerian), Ptah (Egyptian)

THE TRICKSTER

The trickster is a god of trickery, thieving, mischief and can be invoked for playfulness and cheating, but be warned, they may turn their trickery on you! The other pertinent point to note is that the trickster gods are known to cross dress or appear in female form.

Examples are Prometheus (Greek), Loki (Norse)

GODS OF THE UNDERWORLD

The gods of the underworld, although dark are not necessarily evil. They can be invoked to assist with mourning, grief, to force change. They are also often seen as passive and can be used when seeking balance. They can also be invoked for fertility and for getting money.

Examples are Hades (Greek), Pluto (Roman), Osiris (Egyptian), Cernunnos (Celtic), Enmesarra (Sumerian)

COMMON GODDESSES

The goddess is most associated with the moon, thus her symbol is shown as the moon in all its aspects, waxing, full and waning. Her colour is shown as silver.

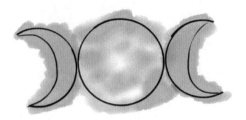

THE GODDESSES OF FERTILITY

The goddesses of fertility are associated with crops, grain and the seasons. They are also often associated with marriage, fertility and childbirth. They can be invoked for fertility, assistance in marriage and marital love.

Examples are Frigg (Norse), Demeter (Greek), Ceres (Roman), Sopdet (Egyptian), Innana (Sumerian)

THE GODDESS OF LOVE

The goddesses of Love can be invoked to bring passionate love and fertility. It must be noted, however that the goddesses of love were not known for fidelity, thus distinguishing them from the goddesses of fertility, who were known to also be the goddesses of marriage.

Examples are Freya (Norse), Aphrodite (Greek), Venus (Roman), Anat (Egyptian)

THE VIRGIN HUNTRESS

The huntress goddesses were primarily virgins, and they were known to be the goddess of the hunt, often associated with the moon. These goddesses are also seen to exhibit masculine traits of strength and focus and are sometimes seen as androgynous and or lesbian. They can be invoked to assist with young women who are still virgins, to assist with chastity but with feminine strength as well.

Examples are Artemis (Greek), Diana (Roman), Neith (Egyptian)

THE TRIPLE GODDESS (MAIDEN, MOTHER, CRONE)

The Triple Goddesses are known as the goddess in her three aspects, as maiden, mother and the crone reflecting the life path of women, and the cycle of the moon. She is often used by witches and represents feminine power, magick and mysticism.

Examples are Brighid (Celtic), Holda (Germanic), Hecate (Greek)

GODDESSES OF THE MOON

The moon goddesses are often associated with woman, and the monthly cycle. They are often seen as the opposite of the sub gods, and are sometimes portrayed as their nemesis. Moon goddesses can be invoked for lunar rituals or spells where balance is required.

Examples are Selene (Greek), Luna (Roman)

DARK GODDESSES

Dark goddesses are not evil, they are seen as keepers of the underworld. They are sometimes there to accompany souls on their final journey. They can be invoked for mourning and chaos.

Examples are Hel (Norse), Epona (Celtic), Ereshkigal (Sumerian), Kauket (Egyptian), Kali (Hindu)

GODDESS OF KNOWLEDGE/ MAGICK

These are goddesses of magick and can be used to assist when doing any kind of magick, but more specifically by women who perform magick. Many of the goddesses of knowledge and magick are also seen as triple goddesses or as goddesses with three aspects.

Examples are Isis (Egyptian), Hecate (Greek), Circe (Greek), Morrigan (Celtic)

THE MYSTERIES

Within covens and the traditional teachings there comes the concept of 'The Mysteries'. The women in the coven are taken aside and taught the women's mysteries and the men are taught the men's mysteries. The mysteries are in effect the magickal uses of the body's reproductive cycle. To give the teachers the benefit of the doubt, I assume this is based on the old traditions where men were excluded from menstruation and birthing and women are kept in dark about sex until after they are married.

Of course in a queer context, this doesn't make much sense because some men menstruate and some women have seminal fluid. Given that queer people have a broad range of relationships with these bodily functions, the standard teachings and associations don't apply. I've renamed the mysteries from the men's mysteries and women's mysteries into a broader more functional description and tailored them to the queer experiences of the mysteries. These are also not limited to be used by people who menstruate or produce seminal fluid. The mysteries are about attuning yourself and being knowledgeable about your cycles.

MONTHLY MYSTERIES

The monthly mysteries are not just for people who menstruate (although they have traditionally been referred to as the women's mysteries). In the traditional binary worldview, the monthly mysteries are based on the ovulation and menstrual cycle. Not all people however have the same experience of ovulation and menstruation. For some people ovulation and menstruation can be a cause of significant distress and dysphoria while other people aren't bothered about it. How you work with your cycle is entirely dependent on your relationship with your body. These are also not limited to people who have menstrual cycles, these associations can also be followed by people who never have or no longer menstruate.

The menstrual cycle is on average 28 days, which coincidentally corresponds with the length of the lunar cycle. Some traditions teach that you should go to all lengths to correspond your cycle with the moon. It is not necessary, but as you can use the cycle of the moon to determine the timing of specific spells and working, so you can also use the menstrual cycle to determine the type of spells and workings. Because magick is driven from emotion, you may find that you have particular strong associations with the cycle (or parts of it) and this may lead you to not ever use the cycle in workings. You also have the option of working these out for yourself, spend time tracking your monthly cycle and how you feel in each of the phases. This tracking is not limited to people who menstruate.

You can track you emotions through an average month and work out where your cycle would be. Then use those emotions to drive what your own spell associations are.

WEEK ONE

Stage: New Beginnings
Menstrual Cycle: Pre-Ovulation
Moon: Dark Moon to Waxing Moon

This is typically a week where you will feel full of hope. During this week your focus should be on taking action to start new endeavours. It's a good time to sign up for training, updating your CV or going for interviews. This is the time for any growth spells that are associated with starting something new; these should be spells for a new job, new home or love spells.

WEEK TWO

Stage: Fertility and Growth
Menstrual Cycle: Ovulation
Moon: Waxing to Full Moon

This will be a week where the plans that you have laid in the previous week start taking shape. It's a good time to be very productive and get things done. This is the time for success spells, and spells for growth. These should be spells that are seeing the plans put in place ready come to fruition.

WEEK THREE

Stage: Contemplation and Planning
Menstrual Cycle: Pre-menstruation
Moon: Full to Waning Moon

The third week is often linked to periods of high stress, frustration and anger. It is a time when the plans you've put in place and worked on in the previous week have either come to fruition or failed. It can be a very trying time full of high emotions. It is often a time associated with letting go of things and releasing control. It is a time of reflection and contemplation. If you are following a cycle, it is the time when you consider your options and start thinking about what plans you will need to put in place for the coming cycle. It's a good time for divination.

WEEK FOUR

Stage: Getting rid of negativity
Menstrual Cycle: Menstruation
Moon: Waning moon to Dark Moon

This week is a time often associated with being tired and things coming to an end. You may feel tired, depressed or particularly dysphoric at this time. This is the week to cast spells to get rid of anything negativity and bad influences. It's also a good time to give up any bad habits that you have. There are some scholars that teach that the menstrual blood is particularly potent for these sorts of spells, however you need to be cautious about its use. An example of this is to use menstrual blood for a protection spell to drive out harmful or hurtful energies from the home, and the menstrual blood is mixed with herbs for protection (such as bay leaf or rosemary) and then buried in the ground. This is of course not advised if there is a risk of it being dug up by animals in the area.

ORGASM MYSTERIES

Once again, the orgasm mysteries are not only for those who produce seminal fluid (even though in tradition these have been called the men's mysteries). The principle of the orgasm mysteries is that masturbation is a form of raising a significant amount of energy, culminating in the orgasm where the release is the apex point where the energy is directed and focused at what the spell is for. This way of raising energy and directing a spell can be used for any spells where a significant amount of force is required to accomplish a goal; it is less well suited for spells where a softer, gentler energy is used. Once again, it is possible to use the fluids that arise from the raising of energy to add to the spell and any fluids buried in the ground. Once again, this is not advised if there is a risk of it being dug up by animals in the area.

THE ELEMENTS

In paganism, it is often believed that everything in the universe is made up of the five elements namely, spirit, earth, air, water and fire. This does not conflict with modern scientific theory; rather it is seen as a spiritual base, not a scientific one. The origins of these elements, known as the classical elements have been used in various cultures for example, the early Greeks and Hindus. Interestingly, if one looks at the scientific states of matter and adds combustion as a state, one could classify them as follows:

- Solid state - Earth element
- Liquid state - Water element
- Gaseous state - Air element
- Combustion state - Fire element

Each element is associated with a cardinal direction such as North, East, South, and West. It is important to remember that the symbolic meaning is associated to the element.

The elements are also knows as quarters or watchtowers.

REPRESENTATIONS OF THE ELEMENTS

The representations of the elements are a subjective thing. The associations need to be felt, not learned from a book. All magick is fuelled by emotion, and can only be learned from experience.

To experience the emotion associated with an element, you will need to spend time with in, get to know it, understand its purpose and become its friend.

Choose the first element you want to work with. If, for example, you choose the element of earth, Find a spot of unspoiled beauty of land, for example in your garden, and spend some time there. If it is possible, spend an hour or two a day or week in the garden. Just sit in silence and watch the earth, feel the emotions it evokes within you. Think of words to describe these emotions, and use these in your invocations.

Once you have completed this element you can move onto the next one. For fire, try using a bonfire or a candle, for water, the ocean, a waterfall, or even a pond for air try going to a windy place, out in the open.

Try to find the elements in their natural environment, meditating on a glass of water probably won't give you the same results as a pond or fountain would. At first, it is important to try to focus on one element at a time, so that you don't confuse the emotions, but as you become more familiar with the elements you will be able to pick out emotions from experiences you have. If you go on holiday to the mountains or the sea, you may find that you emotions associated to the earth or water elements will change. For example, I always know that earth was a nourishing and sustaining element, but I also felt it was rather unglamorous, lacking the vitality and power of fire, until I did a handfasting in the Drakensburg mountains in South Africa. As I looked up to call the element of earth, I was struck by the absolute power, strength and majesty of the mountains. It changed the way I saw the earth element significantly.

The symbols of the elements can be carved into the quarter candles, or can be used when trying to connect with a specific element. The symbols show an equilateral triangle as male (the phallus) and the upside down equilateral triangle as female (the chalice).

EARTH

In the Greek Classical elements, the element of earth is seen as representing material possessions and the physical realm. Earth is strong and stable as well as its role as nourishing plants and sustaining life must be taken into consideration. Earth, when controlled can direct air (wind must blow around a mountain), put out fires, and channel water (think of a river). Earth is represented by the colour Green.

Because of the nourishing and sustaining forces of this element, this element is seen as a positive polarity (or female) element.

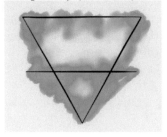

AIR

Air is associated with the powers of the mind such as intellect, swift though and communication because airflow cannot be stopped, it can only be directed. Once directed, air is a powerful force, able to move earth (think of a dust storm), put out (or feed) fire, and shift the waters (think of the ocean waves). Air is represented by the colour Yellow.

Because of the intellectual (as opposed to emotional) aspects of this element, this element is seen as a negative polarity (or male) element.

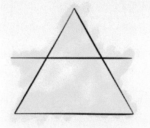

WATER

In the Greek classical elements, water represents the soul and the emotions because of its changeable nature. Water moves, and affects all those in its path, when standing in a stream, water will move past you, but you will get wet. Water has the power to douse fires; water can dilute earth, and in so doing can consume it. Water is represented by the colour blue.

Because of its emotive qualities, Water is a positive polarity (or female) element.

FIRE

Fire represents of passion, desire and creativity. Fire can also represent anger or hatred because it has the power to destroy everything in its path. Fire, can be used to create, for instance the fire in a blacksmith's forge, it can be used to propel, for example combustion engines. Although fire can be used to direct anger and hatred, the fire soon consumes its fuel and will burn itself out. Fire can destroy all the other elements if it is large enough. It will evaporate water, consume the air and scorch the earth. Fire is represented by the colour red.

Fire is uncontrolled passion, creativity and possibly destruction, thus it is seen as a negative polarity (or male) element.

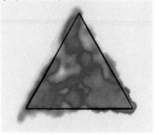

SPIRIT

There is an additional element which is also referenced which is the element of spirit. This element represents the life force that is within all living things, and is also sometimes seen as the soul. The elements are not specifically represented on the altar or in the circle as the element is always present when you are. The symbols for spirit is the symbol of the combined elements, and is often associated with purple.

THE PENTAGRAM

Before proceeding it is worth mentioning a common symbol used for paganism is the pentagram. One of the most common symbols is the pentagram. The corners of the pentagram represent the four classical elements with the fifth element of spirit, in the right way round pentagram the spirit element is on top, and is therefore seen to be in control of the other elements.

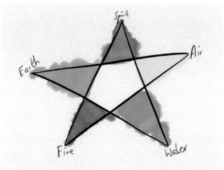

The inverted pentagram is also often used as symbol of Satanism, although in pagan terms means that the element of spirit is no longer in control.

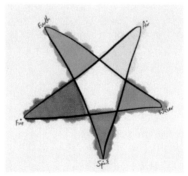

THE PENTACLE

The pentacle is a pentagram within a circle and represents the five elements working in harmony (within a sacred circle) and is seen as unifying the power of the five elements.

POSITIONS OF THE ELEMENTS IN A RITUAL OR CIRCLE

The placing of the elements must be relative to your position on the planet. Fire should always be in the direction of the equator because that is where the largest body of fire (the sun) is the closest, either north (Southern Hemisphere) or south (Northern Hemisphere). Directly opposite Fire must be the other negative polarity element Air, either north or south depending on where Fire is.

That leaves the two positive polarity elements. This is a bit more relative to your exact location. You need to look at where the closest body of water is relative to where you are either east or west. Thus, the final element is Earth, opposite Water.

This is not an exact science; you just need to place them where it makes sense to you. Most of magick is about what feels right. If it doesn't feel right it's not going to work for you.

This places the quarters differently to how is often prescribed by Wiccan and Pagan books, but the explanation is as follows: If the elements, being positive or negatively charged, are thought of as magnetic polarities, it would not make sense to place two of the same polarities next to each other. However, if you place the elements in an order of positive-negative-positive-negative there would be constant movement as the elemental energies are attracted to one another they would start to spin. This spinning is similar to what happens in a generator or electric motor, which causes energy to build. These diagrams may show you what I mean.

Here is a diagram showing the forces in a circle with the traditional element positions:

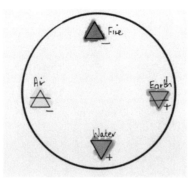

This causes the elements to move to a position similar to this, and the circle collapses:

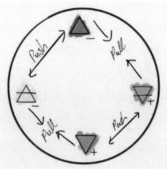

However, if you place the elements positive-negative-positive-negative your movement will be like this:

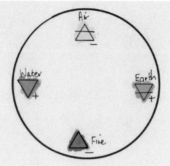

The direction of the movement, either widdershins (anti-clockwise) or deosil (clockwise) is dictated by the direction that the energy flows in when you cast your circle and the order that you call the quarters in.

WIDDERSHINS OR DEOSIL

Deosil is considered the 'right' way, for doing rituals for good things, like drawing things toward you, and widdershins is the direction you use when doing 'negative' workings, for example a banishing. Coming from southern Africa these was quite a bit of confusion about which direction to work in in the southern hemisphere, so we've included a detailed explanation here.

Before knowing which to use, widdershins or deosil, we must first understand what each word means. It is generally accepted that deosil means clockwise and widdershins means anticlockwise. This is true, but only for the Northern hemisphere. You see, Deosil means 'sun wise', and thus in the southern hemisphere, this would be classed and clockwise. Widdershins means 'opposite course' and thus it would mean anticlockwise in the Northern Hemisphere.

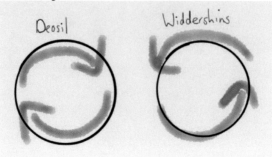

However, cross over the equator, and what happens? Deosil becomes anticlockwise, and Widdershins becomes clockwise. Thus if you want to work Deosil, follow the sun relative to your geographic location. Thus in South Africa and Australia, for example, Deosil is anticlockwise and widdershins is clockwise.

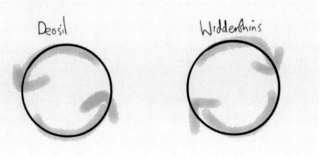

DAYS OF THE WEEK

MONDAY

Colours: Silver
Planet: The Moon
Astrology: Cancer, Pisces
Polarity: Positive
Crystals: Moonstone, Opal

Monday is the day of the moon, and it represents being in contact with the feminine divine and is a good day for deepening the spiritual meaning of your relationships and home life. This day is also a good day for scrying and foretelling the future. Monday influences dreams, emotions, clairvoyance, home, family, medicine, cooking, personality, merchandising and theft.

TUESDAY

Colours: Red
Planet: Mars
Astrology: Aries
Polarity: Negative
Crystals: Bloodstone, Garnet

This is a day for strength, passion, righteous anger and courage. Tuesday is a good day for rituals to protect and assist people in unfair situations. Tuesday influences dynamic energy, matrimony, war, enemies, prison, hunting, surgery, courage, politics and contests.

WEDNESDAY

Colours: Yellow
Planet: Mercury
Astrology: Gemini, Virgo
Polarity: Negative
Crystals: Citrine, Yellow Jasper

Wednesday is a day for harmonising, healing, guidance, a deeper understanding of spiritual knowledge, alleviating worries of daily life and for teaching. Wednesday influences communication, reason, divination, skill, debt, fear and self-improvement.

THURSDAY

Colours: Blue
Planet: Jupiter
Astrology: Sagittarius, Scorpio
Polarity: Positive
Crystals: Lapis Lazuli, Turquoise

Thursday is a day of charity, helping others, bringing better harvests, increase abundance and for prosperity. Thursday influences health, honour, luck, riches, clothing, money, legal matters and desires.

FRIDAY

Colours: Green
Planet: Venus
Astrology: Libra, Taurus
Polarity: Positive
Crystals: Jade, Rose Quarts

Fridays represent pure, altruistic love, forgiveness, harmony to places and people. Workings done on Fridays can be for restoring natural balance, for fertility and for any workings for nature and the earth. Friday influences Love, friendship, social activities, strangers, pleasure, art, music, incense and perfumes.

SATURDAY

Colours: Purple
Planet: Saturn
Astrology: Aquarius, Capricorn
Polarity: Neutral
Crystals: Obsidian, Jet

Saturday is the day of solitude, temperance, investment and speculation. It is also a day for moderation and development of inner stillness. This day is good for workings for reversing bad fortune, for conserving resources and keeping things in their natural state. Saturday influences self-discipline, life, building, doctrine, protection, freedom, elderly, destroying diseases and pests.

SUNDAY

Colours: Gold
Planet: The Sun
Astrology: Leo
Polarity: Negative
Crystals: Citrine, Crystal Quartz

This day is one for illumination, inspiration, individuality. This day can be used for creative ventures, new ideas and standing up for what you believe in. Sunday's influences are individuality, hope, fortune, money, work, power, healing, promotion, strength and spirituality.

COLOURS

Colours have a marked impact on people, and this impact can be used when working with anything to do with colour. There are several important points to remember when using colour associations. The lighter range of the colour represents a less intense emotion, and the darker shades of the colour represent a more severe representation. A colour that uses a combination of the colours (for example turquoise) has the association of the combination of those colours (blue and green).

RED

Day: Tuesday
Planet: Mars
Astrology: Aries
Polarity: Negative

Red represents the element of Fire and thus is associated with strength, vigour, lust, and danger. Red is also associated with victory, courage, physical strength, intensity, aggression, energy, force, sexuality and transformation. Because red is also the colour of blood it also represents health, life, birth and war. Red is a negative colour and represents will-power, determination, assertiveness, masculinity, independence, competition and virility.

For healing, red brings warmth, stimulates energy, and is good for the heart and blood circulation. Red is the colour of passion and desire and is thus useful for increasing sexual appetite and for stabilising the menstrual cycle. Red is also said to increase cell production, the functioning of any organ and said to heighten the senses.

ORANGE

Day: Wednesday
Planet: Mercury
Astrology: Gemini
Polarity: Negative

Orange is a combination of the colours Red and Yellow, thus its significance can be drawn from both. Orange lacks the intensity of red, but it adds the intellect and logic of the colour yellow. Because of the mixture of passion (red) and intellect (yellow) orange represents prosperity, abundance, investments, success is business and legal matters. Orange also represents encouragement, adaptation, attraction, stimulation, kindness, charm, optimism, feast and celebration.

For Healing, orange stimulates the lungs, and thus respiration. It also aids in digestion, relieving stomach cramps and muscle spasms. Orange is said to stimulate the thyroid and increase the amount of milk a mother will produce.

YELLOW

Day: Wednesday
Planet: Mercury
Astrology: Virgo
Polarity: Negative

Yellow represents the element of Air and thus represents intellect, knowledge, persuasion, charm, confidence, communication, analysis and memory. Yellow aids students and in learning as it improves concentration and understanding. Yellow is also the colour of the sun and therefore represents the sun, sunlight, creativity, dispelling negative energy, life force, and vitality. Yellow aids in astral projection, telepathy and mental abilities. Yellow aids in business by increasing communication, trade and enables negotiation.

In healing, yellow increases brain activity and assist the nervous system. It also energises the muscles and increases digestion and a healthy bowl. Yellow is also said to aid in lifting depression.

GREEN

Day: Friday
Planet: Venus
Astrology: Libra
Polarity: Positive

Green is the colour that represents earth and thus is known to be associated with fertility, growth, rejuvenation, harmony, nature and the realm of faeries. Green is a positive colour and thus represents charity, recovery, healing, harvest, abundance, peace, and hope. Green is associated as the colour of money and this it represents the finances, prosperity, wealth, luck and success. However, dark green represents greed, envy and jealousy.

In healing, green brings balance to the body, mind and spirit. It can be used to balance any aspect pf the body for example the kidneys, hormones, digestive system and increases immunity. Green also brings growth and builds up muscles, bones and tissues. Green can be used to restore tissue from damage from bacterial infections.

BLUE

Day: Thursday
Planet: Jupiter, Pluto
Astrology: Sagittarius, Scorpio
Polarity: Positive

Blue represents the element of water and as such is seen as tranquil, peaceful, understanding, patient, health, inner peace, harmony, purification and guidance. Blue is a positive colour and it represents truth, honour, sincerity, emotion and protection during sleep or meditation. Blue also brings inspiration, justice and wisdom. The lighter blues represent peace, tranquillity and inner calm especially when doing meditations. The darker blues represent communication, loyalty and creativity.

Blue is very good to use in healing as it calms and soothes fevers, inflammation, irritation, itching, high blood pressure and headaches. Blue also helps to relieve stress.

PURPLE

Day: Saturday
Planet: Saturn
Astrology: Aquarius
Polarity: Neutral

Purple is a combination of blue (water) and red (fire), and represents power, success, idealism, piety, sanctity, tension, wisdom, spirituality and protection. Purple represents the balance between passions and emotions and thus represents justice, the psychic, idealism, guidance and compassion. Purple is seen as a spiritual colour and thus represents divination, prophecy, psychic healing, astral projection, meditation,

When healing with purple, it is a colour of transformation and thus aids in assisting with overcoming depression, addictions and combating stress. It also decreases sensitivity to pain and increases the production of white blood cells, increasing immunity.

BROWN

Day: Friday
Planet: Earth
Astrology: Taurus
Polarity: Positive

Brown is the colour of the earth, the soil beneath our feet and as such it is associated with grounding, trees, pets, animals, material increase, telepathy and animal healing. It is also associated with stability and conservation. Brown aids in concentration, telepathy, protection, justice, retribution and locating things that have been lost.

Brown is often used with Green.

PINK

Day: Saturday
Planet: Saturn
Astrology: Capricorn
Polarity: Positive

Pink is a combination of red (passion and desire) with white (purity) and thus represents a softer kind of love. The associations with pink are family love, romance, friendship, affections, unselfishness, femininity, creativity, marriage, compassion, kindness, and beauty. Pink can be used when doing spiritual healing, working with your inner child and when banishing hatred and negativity.

The darker pinks represent more passion, thus they would represent romance and marriage, where the lighter pinks represent friendship.

WHITE

Day: All
Planet: All
Astrology: All
Polarity: Neutral

Theoretically, white is not a colour, merely the absence of colour. It represents the full moon, purity, meditation, breaking curses, exorcism, healing, peace, cleansing and the highest form of spiritual enlightenment. White represents pure spirit, divination, prophecy, clairvoyance, and contact with higher self and spirit guides. White can be used to replace any other colour.

BLACK

Day: All
Planet: All
Astrology: All
Polarity: Neutral

Black is also not a colour, but rather the absence of light. Thus it absorbs light and energy. Black can be used for banishing evil or negativity, deep meditation, absorption, defensive spells, and removing confusion and clutter from the mind. Black represents self-control, restriction, depression, sickness, new changes, rebirth, wisdom, resilience, discipline and protection.

GREY

Day: Monday
Planet: Neptune
Astrology: Pisces
Polarity: Neutral

Grey is a combination of white and black. Thus it represents balance, neutrality, calm, peace, solitude, patience and neutralising negative energies or emotions. Grey can be used to cancel out situations.

SILVER

Day: Monday
Planet: Moon
Astrology: Cancer
Polarity: Positive

Silver is the colour of the full moon, represents the Goddess aspect and thus the feminine divine. Silver represents purity, values, treasure and the unconscious mind. Silver can be used for any form of divination, dispelling negativity and protection. Because of the influence of the moon, silver can cause emotions to become strong and intense and caution must be taken when using silver with people who are mentally or emotionally unstable.

GOLD

Day: Sunday
Planet: Sun
Astrology: Leo
Polarity: Negative

Gold represents the Sun and the God. Thus it is also used to represent energy, warmth, virility, wealth, financial wisdom, activity, intelligence, intellect, the mind, analysis, memory and creativity. Gold can be used to represent financial wealth, prosperity, richness and investments.

11. MAGICKAL TOOLS

As has been discussed in various parts, your subconscious is probably the most powerful tool that you have at your disposal. This is one of the main reasons why a magickal tool must only be used for magickal purposes and not for mundane ones. When you purchase or make a tool, there is a certain amount of intent in it, irrespective of how long it takes to find or to make the tool. With that intent, your subconscious mind is preparing itself for what the purpose of that tool will be, and you have started to charge the tool before you even have it.

When you find the tool, or the tool has been completed, your subconscious mind associates all the thoughts you had about making or buying that tool (this is one of the reasons why you should never haggle over price of a tool). There are certain associations that some tools have which traditionally denote the masculine and feminine aspects. These can be crudely described as being the phallic shape (sword, athame, wand) as the masculine which is giving off energy (as the phallus projects sperm) and the bowl or receptacle shape (bowl, cup, chalice) is seen as the receiver of the energy (as the womb receives the sperm). The combination of these is used to represent creation (as the conception of a child).

Before using any tool, it must be cleansed, consecrated and charged. This is to remove any energy that may have been in the tool before it came into your possession. This also applies when making a tool. For example, when making a tool from wood, you need to remove all the energy that is in the wood from the process of planting, cutting, transporting and selling that piece of wood. The tool must also be consecrated; this means that it must be made fit for sacred space. The last part of the tool preparation is the charging. The tool must be charged with your energy, and your intent. This seals the tool's purpose in your subconscious mind, and every time you use the tool, it more firmly embeds the tools purpose in your mind.

When you use your magickal tool for mundane things, your subconscious mind adds those things to that tools purpose. For example, you have a pair of running shoes, you only use these shoes for running, and you run every day. When you put these shoes on, your subconscious mind starts preparing your body for the upcoming run. Then one day, you use your shoes for working in the garden. The next time you put your shoes on, your subconscious mind becomes confused, because it can't figure out if you're going running or doing gardening. Although this may be a very crude example, the principle is the same. You need to ensure that your subconscious undoubtedly knows what that tool is for.

It is important to remember the role of the tools in workings; the tool is not the only thing that makes the magick work. Dion Fortune, in her book called Applied Magick (Fortune, 1979), says:

"If we understand the psychology of ritual we shall neither be in bondage to superstition nor in rebellion against empty forms. We shall realise that a form is the channel for a force but it is not only the material substance used in sacrament, which is the physical channel for a force, but also the vivid pictorial image created in the mind of the worshipper by its ritual use"

This means that you must always bear in mind that any tool you use in ritual is a channel for a force, but the tool itself does not channel the force, rather the combination of the symbolic function of the tool and the image in your imagination that created the channel for that force.

A good place to find magickal tools is markets, second-hand shops or esoteric shops. However, it is important that you do not quibble over the price, because you must pay what the item is worth, and not place material values and money above your spiritual practices. If you cannot afford an item, it may not be the right tool for you. You may find that money is the obstacle placed in your way to get you to wait for something better. Before you start looking for a tool, ask your chosen deities for the tool, and be specific, ask for it by shape, size and approximate price, and you will find your tool much easier.

THE ALTAR

Traditionally an altar is a place where sacrifices are offered to deity. In Paganism, however, the altar is a working space. The Altar becomes your focal point during the ritual as well as it is often used as a working space. The tools and things that you will use on your Altar should only be used for magickal purposes and not in the mundane world. Practically, this allows you to either have a running Altar all the time or have your Altar tools packed together to find them easier.

The Altar itself should be low enough for you to work at while kneeling or sitting. It should be made of a natural substance such as wood, stone or ceramic that will work well with the energies of the circle. The altar should only be used as an altar and should not be used for mundane purposes once it has been consecrated. However, it is often not practical to have a running altar set up all the time, and in this case you would need to consecrate each time you use it for magick.

A common altar is a medium sized coffee table, but if you do not have a table to use in ritual, you can lay an Altar cloth on the floor and use that as an Altar. Other ideas for altars are things such as a flat piece of rock, or a tree stump or log. There are very effective when doing outdoor rituals, and if you have one of these an altar cloth may not be necessary.

The Altar must be a representation of your sacred space, and therefore should be a representation of the sacredness of the outside world, thus it should have deity and the five elements. Traditionally the Altar has two much defined sides, the male side and the female side. On the male side you would have all your male representation for example the God statue and the incense, on the female side you would have the Goddess statue and the bowls with the water and salt. Remember, as long as you believe in what you are doing, your altar can be set up in any way you like.

This is a very basic layout of an altar:

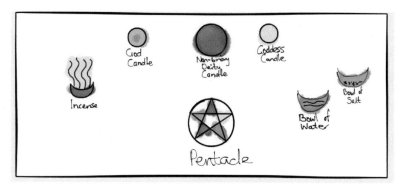

AN ALTAR CLOTH

Some people like to use Altar cloths of varying colours on their Altars. An Altar cloth is simply a tablecloth that is used on the Altar. It is essential that your Altar cloth not be flammable, because you will be working with fire (the incense and candles) on your Altar and you do not want to set it alight.

A collection of Altar cloths is a nice thing to start because you may want different colours for different workings. A good start is to get one white and one black Altar cloth, and then to start collecting other colours at each Sabbat, which is every eight weeks. This will lead to an extensive collection of colours by the end of that year, and it is not harsh on the budget.

DEITY STATUES

On the Altar there should be a representation of deity. A good idea is to get a deity statues or set of deity statues small enough to fit on the Altar that works for you. These can be anything from actual statues from your chosen pantheon, to symbolic statues of the masculine, feminine and non-binary divine. Other things that can be used as deity representation on the altar are stones, shells, feathers or bone. It is important to get something that will mean something to you, because it is your focal point for your deity concept.

PENTACLE

The pentacle is a representative of the material world, and the element of earth. Thus it is has a positive polarity. It has also been associated with the coins deck of the tarot cards.

The pentacle is also the name given to a pentagram with a star around it (see the magickal symbols section). For the use as a tool, a pentacle is something with a drawn, burned or carved pentacle on it.

The pentacle is usually in the centre, near the front of the Altar, because this is where the working will occur. You use the pentacle as a working surface for any workings that need to be done. For example when you need to cleanse and consecrate a new tool, you would place it on the pentacle when you cleanse it. The pentacle should be made of a natural material, preferable wood or clay, and should not be more than half or smaller than a quarter of the size of the Altar.

CENSURE AND INCENSE

Incense is used in ritual to represent the negative elements of fire and air; therefore it has a negative polarity.

Plants have certain magickal associations, and uses and when incense is made of the plant, the magickal associations are carried over into the incense. When you smell the scent of incense, certain triggers in your brain and subconscious associate that smell with certain things. This helps to set your intent for the ritual. The incense also adds to the energy that is raised and used in circle and is often used as a driving force in spells. There are two types of incense most commonly used; these are loose incense and stick incense.

Stick incense is the commercially available incense sticks. There are many types of censures available for stick incense. It is important to choose the incense that has the appropriate aroma for your specific ritual. It is also preferable to get stick incense that states what the aroma is as opposed to choosing one that is branded under a specific name. For example, it is better to get sandalwood incense than incense called 'dreaming', because it ensures that the fragrance will link up to your intent.

For those who are fortunate enough to have dried herbs freely available, you can make your own incense. Loose incense can also be bought from esoteric shops and stalls, however once again make sure you know what's in it. You will then need coals and a censure for coals. An easy censure is to get a bowl that you can place sand in. Then place the lit coal on the sand and place the incense on top of it. It is a good idea to get a pair of tongs (like the ones they use for sugar cubes) to hold the coal while you light it.

It is important to have extra incense on the altar for during the ritual, whether you are using stick or loose incense. Also make sure that you or any others in your circle are not allergic to anything in the incense or the incense itself. If someone is allergic, don't use incense at all.

BOWL OF WATER AND BOWL OF SALT

The bowl of water and the bowl of salt are representative of the elements of earth and water. Holy water can be made rather simply by adding a drop or two of rose oil to the water. Either coarse or refined sea salt can be used, depending on your personal preference. I personally prefer to use a mixture of course and refined sea salt, with a lavender head and a sprig of rosemary in.

CHALICE & BOWL

The chalice and bowl are there for the cakes and ale part of the ritual (see the ritual section). These are both, by their shape, representative of the female divine. The contents (the cake and ale) can be considered as the product of the union of the God and Goddess.

BOLINE AND ATHAME

A Boline and an Athame are both double bladed knives, no longer than the inside of your arm, from inside the elbow to the tip of your middle finger. They are associated with the element of air, the tarot suit of swords or knives and therefore representative of the masculine divine.

The Boline is white handled and used for cutting things in the physical plane that will be used for magick, for example harvesting herbs, or carving a piece of wood. The Athame on the other hand is a dark handled knife that used for cutting on the spiritual plane and for projecting energy through, for example, casting the circle or cutting a portal in the circle. Both the Boline and the Athame represent the male divinity.

A sword is an Athame longer than the inside of your forearm and is used in the same way as an Athame. When using a sword to cast the circle, it is common for the sword to be dragged on the ground to show the physical demarcation of the circle.

STAFF OR WAND

The wands are usually made of wood and represent the male aspect of divinity. The staff is a larger version of a wand. Traditionally the wand is no longer than the inside of your arm from elbow to wrist. The staff is anything longer than that, and is usually shoulder height. Both the wand and the staff are used for the same purposes as the Athame or sword.

BROOM/ BESOM

The Besom is a broom used on the spiritual plane, and is used for cleansing an area before casting a circle. It is used in much the same way as an ordinary broom, except the bristles do not touch the ground, to symbolically sweep away any negative or resident energy from that area. The Besom is often used in house cleansings.

In older traditions the besom should be made from an Ash tree, however these are often difficult to find, so any broom made of all natural materials can be used. The Besom, like the other tools should only be used for sacred work and not for mundane cleaning.

BELL

The Bell is a goddess symbol, because of its shape and can be rung when invoking or devoking deity and also to signify the end of a spell or working.

CAULDRON

The cauldron is representative of the Goddess's womb, and thus a female symbol and the symbol of water. It is usually used in workings where a potion is being created, although it can also be used for burning pieces of paper etc. in when these are involved in a working. Some people also use the cauldron to make a fire in when they do not have a fire pit.

ROBES

Your robes are your 'church clothes' or 'Sunday best', this is what you wear when you are in contact with deity. What you wear says something to you, how you feel about yourself and how others see you. Thus you need to wear something that shows you reverence and respect both for yourself and the deity that you will be meeting. Robes also have the effect of casting of your mundane self and embracing your spiritual self. You prepare yourself mentally for ritual, while you are preparing physically.

A lot of people like to use long flowing robes that allow freedom of movement and expression. Traditionally your robes should be of a natural fibre (again, not flammable), and should be made by you. Robes are the alternative offered to going skyclad (naked). In some traditions you are not allowed to face deity unless you are naked, signifying that you have nothing to hide. Nowadays, we have a more progressive view and if you are doing a private ritual and everyone consents and is over the legal age, people can go skyclad, but it is more generally accepted to wear either street clothes, or robes.

Traditionally, you should be naked under your robe, with no make-up, perfume, or hair products on. If you have long hair you should leave it hanging loose without a clip, hair elastic etc. It is believed that your hair has great power, and you should not restrain your power in any way. In some traditions you may not enter the circle with any form of clothing on. The reasoning behind this is that being sky clad represents that you have separated yourself from the physical world and are now operating on the spiritual plane, although this can be uncomfortable for some. If you have a set of robes or clothing specifically for ritual you will find that you associate those clothes with spirituality and after a while, just putting them on will help prepare you for the ritual to come.

Ritual is also a time where you can express yourself and live outside of the social boundaries; you are meeting with the divine on your own terms. If that means that you choose to dress flamboyantly and wear make-up that is your choice, you are showing deity the core of your being, you are using this time to discover more about yourself and how you fit in within the divine energies of the universe, if that means you are most comfortable in nothing but a burlap sack it is no less valid than being in 9-inch heels and false eyelashes. It is important though to remember that you are dressing for you. It is worth noting however that if you are running the ritual with other people, be sure to set the expectations. Some of the traditional values of no make-up, no hair ties etc. still hold sway.

THE BELT

The belt in a coven is a symbol of rank. A single cord usually means that you have joined the coven, but have not been passed the first degree yet, at first degree and the subsequent degrees the members each get a new cord to add to their belts. Usually there are a maximum of five belts, and these are worn by the elders of the coven.

CANDLES

At the minimum, there are usually three candles on my altar, a God candle, a Goddess candle and the Universal candle. The Universal candle should be situated between the God and Goddess candles. The candles should correspond with the colours representative of the deities as follows:

- God – Gold
- Goddess – Silver
- Universal – Gold and Silver or White or Black

If you are working at night, you can place nondescript white candles on the altar to use for light so that you can see what you are doing.

QUARTER CANDLES

Quarter candles are used to demarcate the quarters and the outer perimeter of the circle, or if you chose to, you can keep them on the altar. The quarter candles should either be white or the corresponding colours of the quarters. The corresponding colours are:

- Water – Blue
- Earth – Green
- Fire – Red
- Air - Yellow

CUSHIONS

Although these are not really magickal tools, you may find it useful to have a cushion or two near the altar for you to kneel or sit on while you are working at the altar. It is a good idea to have specific cushions that are only used for ritual. These should also be cleansed and consecrated to make them fit for sacred space.

VASE & FLOWERS

The vase with flowers is not an essential, but it is a nice touch and makes your altar visually appealing. It also acts as a nice reminder of the power and beauty of nature. The vase as a vessel is symbol of water and the feminine divine.

LIGHTER/MATCHES

Remember to have at least one lighter or box of matches either on your altar, or with you to light the incense and the candles.

PEN AND PAPER

A pen and wad of paper is usually kept for magickal uses only. This pen and paper are blessed, cleansed and consecrated like any other tool and are therefore not used for mundane purposes.

Certain workings may call for writing something on a piece of paper, and then (for example) throwing it into the fire. The pen and paper should be kept for magickal uses only, just as you would with any other tool.

BOOK OF SHADOWS/ GRIMOIRE

Many traditions of paganism call for a person to have a book of shadows. This is not essential, but is a nice way to keep record.

There are various types of magickal record keeping things, and you need to choose a way that suits you. Some choose and electronic Grimoire, some a file that contains printed or handwritten copies of all the information, and some keep an ordinary A4 book, and others keep a handmade book that has everything handwritten. The types of record keeping books are as follows:

MAGICKAL DIARY

A magickal diary is a place where you keep record of your personal experience of what a specific working or ritual was like. Similar to any other diary, however, the magickal diary only contains entries about magickal things. For example, after a ritual you may want to express the feelings you had before, during and after the ritual.

BOOK OF SHADOWS

A Book of shadows is usually a collection of rituals and workings that you performed. This will include any rituals or workings you have written yourself or attended. In older traditions, the Book of Shadows is a book that contains all the knowledge of the group and handed down to the members, either the book as a whole or the members of the group rewrite the book by hand into their own books.

GRIMOIRE

These days, a Grimoire and Book of Shadows are used interchangeably. However, traditionally a Grimoire is a single book that has the rituals and workings, the knowledge and the diary in a single book.

Section 6:
Ritual

12. RITUAL

A ritual is a formal working where one meets with deity, and the elements in sacred space to perform a working. A working can be a spell, a ceremony, a meditation, divination, a celebration or anything that you feel needs to be performed in sacred space.

A ritual is a chance to break away from the mundane world and walk amongst the pure elements and your chosen deity. It can be a time of relaxation, a time of healing and restfulness or a time of celebration and happiness. It is also a time when you can be exactly who you are, no need for labels, no need to conform and no need to explain who you are to broader society. You are the whole of your essence, with no barriers, disguises and no coverings. You are naked before the divine.

Ritual needs to be something you look forward to and enjoy, if you're getting tired of doing ritual, stop for a while. Take a break, and attempt it again when you're feeling inspired. Ritual is a form of art, you need to have the motivation and inspiration to want to do it otherwise it means nothing to you or the other people involved. You can work hard in ritual, but it must never be work. Your inspiration should carry you and motivate you.

There is no 'good' or 'bad' ritual in the general sense. A good ritual is one where it works, and does what you expect it to, a bad ritual is one that has unexpected or unpleasant results.

During ritual, you are calling upon energy as you experience it. The energy itself has all (and therefore none) of the qualities we, as people, assign to them. For example, if you see fire as destructive and therefore bad, does the fire know that it is bad? Does the fire stop being destructive because you believe it is bad? Of course not. Fire is just that, Fire. It cares not if it is being used to cook food and offer warmth for a family, or if it is burning the family's house down. Fire is just fire. It does not have a moral code of conduct declaring when it will be fire and when it will be something else. All energy is exactly the same. Energy used to summon demons is no different than the energy used to heal. The work that you choose that energy to do is up to you, in much the same way that what you choose to do with fire is up to you. But remember the consequences; at the very least you will get back what you give out.

The ritual, as I have outlined below is my personal way of working, and the way that I have seen many people work. This does not mean that it is cast in stone, and it does not make it the right, or the only way, it is just the way that I prefer. When you start with rituals, try changing the format and order that you use. Leave parts out and add parts in as you feel fit, and find a way that works for you.

THE MAKINGS OF A RITUAL

The following section discusses the practical things to consider when setting up or planning a ritual. It must be noted that a ritual is not necessarily a large group event, a single person can do a ritual by themselves to either do a spell for a specific outcome, to mark an occasion (such as the wheel of the year or the lunar cycle) or even just to take some time out to think and reflect. It can be used to banish negative energies, do readings or just to find peace. Rituals do not need to be hugely elaborate affairs either, they can be just a small token or candle at each quarter with a single item as a focus.

RITUAL SPACE FOR ONE

The outline below of a full ritual can be done for one or many people, but you may find that it becomes cumbersome to use the full ritual outline when doing a ritual for yourself. Try this simple technique to create your sacred space when you either don't have time or don't want to use the full ritual.

Sit, stand or lie comfortably in a space that you have set aside for ritual. Visualise your aura around you, feel the energy flowing through your body. Visualise your aura growing as you feel the energy coursing through you.

While you visualise you can chant the invocation used for the circle cast, either softly to yourself or out loud. Visualise expanding your aura until it forms a workable circle around you. Thus your sacred space is cast.

You can now call quarters and deity if you choose or just work in the circle with your personal energy. If you choose to call the quarters and deity, you can stay where you are and visualise each element, and then the deity entering the circle. Our can chant the invocations as you do this to assist with the visualisation.

POSITION OF THE ALTAR

The altar can be anywhere in the circle that suits you. It makes sense to have the altar near the starting point of your circle casting and quarter calling (at East, North or North-East) because you won't be running up and down to the circle trying to get between the altar and other points of the circle.

More traditionally you can place the altar at East because that's where the Sun rises, at West, because that's where it sets or in the centre to be able to move around it. Make sure that wherever you place your altar it has enough space behind it for you to walk for when you cast the circle, and call the quarters.

PREPARING THE SACRED SPACE

The preparation of for the ritual is almost as important as the ritual itself. While you carry out all the menial tasks required setting and preparing the sacred space you are filling it with your intent. If you are irritated and lazy, you won't have a beautiful peaceful ritual and it will probably fall flat. In ritual, as it is in most of life, what you put in is what you get out.

PREPARING YOUR PERSON

I have put this chapter and the end of the preparation, as this is the most convenient time for me. I find that there is nothing better after lugging things around and preparing the circle space that to take a quick rejuvenating bath or shower and then dressing in my clean fresh robes and preparing myself mentally for the ritual.

During this time it's important not only to get physically refreshed but also to ground yourself of all excess energy and enter the circle with a calm reflective attitude. It's important not to try and get rid of all the emotion, but conserve the emotion and the energy for your invocations and energy raising, don't waste it on mundane things. The cleansing before a ritual is not to rid yourself of sinfulness, but rather to prepare yourself consciously for the ritual.

THE RITUAL ITSELF

Once you have done the preparation, the ritual itself becomes a lot easier. This is the part where your physical work is over and the spiritual work has begun. This is the time where you commune with the spiritual realm. For many, this is the hardest part, because they are scared that nothing is happening or that they will fumble and do the wrong thing. The most important part of ritual and magickal work is confidence. As long as you are confident in what you are doing, you will believe in it and it will become real. If you don't see or feel energy, just focus and believe and that will be enough to bring the energy forth.

Focus is something essential to most magickal workings and the same applies to ritual. Focus on what you are doing at each step; forget about the previous steps and the future ones. If you fumble your words, or forget to light the appropriate candle, either keep going or stop and fix it. Remember, everyone fumbles at some point, no one always does everything perfectly.

Another point to make when doing anything magickal is to be yourself, if you can't memorise long flowing lines and invocations, don't. Just remember the essential parts and use them. Practice saying the words beforehand and practice visualising the energy, while saying the words. If you mess it up, it's not the end of the world. Just remain calm, confident and keep going.

During the ritual, when you have finished an invocation, say, 'So mote it be' or 'By my will, it is done'. This is an equivalent to the Christian 'Amen'. The purpose of this is simply to tell people in the circle that that part is finished so the next can begin, but it also affirms that it has been done. For example, when you bless, cleans and consecrate the elements, you say the invocation that cleanses the element and then by saying 'So mote it be' or 'By my will it is done' you are saying 'This element is now fit to serve in sacred space'.

BLESSING, CLEANSING AND CONSECRATING

Light all the illumination candles, so that you can see what you are doing. Do not light any of the deity candles or the elemental candles yet. Place more incense on the coal, or light another incense stick. The elements on the altar need to be blessed before the ritual can start. This is not necessarily removing all negativity, but rather retuning the element for the work that it is about to do.

While you bless each element, visualise that element in its purest form. Visualise any residual energies leaving the elements and the elements becoming pure. Remember, the elements on the altar are there to represent their greater forms.

Bless the water by placing the tip of the blade of your Athame in the water saying:

> I bless, cleanse and consecrate you, child of water
> That you may be fit to serve in sacred space
> So mote it be

Then place the tip of the Athame in the Salt saying:

> I bless, cleanse and consecrate you, child of earth
> That you may serve in sacred space
> So mote it be

Take a small amount of salt on the tip of your Athame, and place it in the water.

You then bless the fire element by placing the tip of the blade onto the coal (if you are using loose incense) or on the flame of an illumination candle and say the following:

> I bless, cleanse and consecrate you, child of fire
> That you may be fit to serve in sacred space
> So mote it be

Then if using loose incense, place more incense on the coal or use the already lit incense stick. Place the Athame in the smoke that arises from the incense and say:

> I bless, cleanse and consecrate you, child of air
> That you may be fit to serve in sacred space
> So mote it be

CIRCLE CAST

Stand at East, where the Sun rises, with your athame in your hand, facing the outside of the circle. Take a moment to visualise what you are about to do. Gather your thoughts and feel the energy rising within you, start pouring the energy toward your athame in your hand. When you are comfortable with the energy you are sending, raise your athame to shoulder level, with your arm straight. This can also be done with your hands up, down, straight out or by dragging the sword or staff along the ground to demarcate the circle. Visualise the energy pouring out of the tip of the blade, or from the toll you are using, or from your hand/s. Now start moving along the barrier of the circle in the direction that your circle will run. Visualise the energy forming the side of a sphere. Don't move too quickly; take slow deliberate steps as you move around. Make sure that you keep visualising the circle forming.

The circle that you cast is not actually a circle, cylinder or cone. It should be a sphere. The sphere should extend both above ground and below, forming a bubble that you will be enclosed in. The wall of the circle should allow only love in and love out.

The following simple invocation can be used when casting the circle in spirit:

> I cast this circle by my will and by my spirit,
>
> That none but love shall enter
>
> That none but love shall pass

Repeat this invocation as you cast the circle. When you are back at East, stop, facing toward the outside of the circle, with your athame outstretched before you in both hands. Visualise the start and stopping points of the circle you have cast, joining and closing. Now, lower your athame, turn to the centre of the circle and say:

> So mote it be

Now go to the altar, take the bowl with the water and salt in and move back to East. In a similar manner to casting the circle in spirit, you now cast the circle in water and earth saying the following invocation as you move around:

> I cast this circle with the sacred elements of earth and water,
>
> That none but love shall enter
>
> That none but love shall pass

When you have completed the casting in earth and water, turn to the centre of the circle and say:

> So mote it be

Move back to the altar, put the bowl of water down and pick up the censer. Be careful, it may be hot. Walk the perimeter of the circle saying:

> I cast this circle with the sacred elements of fire and air,
> That none but love shall enter
> That none but love shall pass

When you have completed the casting in fire and air, turn to the centre of the circle and say:

> So mote it be

You now place the censer back on the altar.

ELEMENTAL CALLING

The elemental energies are called into a circle to strengthen the circle, and to add to the energy.

The invocations of the elements are very similar, so I will explain it here and then give you a set of standard invocations that I like to use. Start at East where the sun rises.

Stand at the quarter facing out of the circle. Visualise the element that you are calling, feel the emotions that that element evokes within you. Visualise the element coming closer and closer until it is in your circle, while you recite the invocation. Once you are finished invoking the element, light the elemental candle and walk to the next quarter, in the same direction as the circle cast.

Water

> Creative Element of Water,
> Great Spirit of the ocean,
> Hear me as I call you into the East.
> Bring into our circle, Cleansing and Healing
> Spirit of Water!
> Hail and Welcome!

Fire

>Powerful Element of Fire,
>Great Spirit of courage,
>Hear me as I call you into the North.
>Bring into our circle, Passion and desire.
>Spirit of Fire!
>Hail and Welcome!

Earth

>Sustaining Element of Earth,
>Great Spirit of wisdom,
>Hear me as I call you into the West.
>Bring into our circle Strength and Wisdom.
>Spirit of Earth!
>Hail and Welcome!

Air

>Inspiring Element of Air,
>Great Spirit of the mind,
>Hear me as I call you into the South.
>Bring into our circle Movement and Change.
>Spirit of Air!
>Hail and Welcome!

When you have completed invoking the quarters, walk back to the altar.

DEITY CALLING

Invoking deity is not always done. You can choose if you want to or not. I find that invoking the deity is a symbolic way of honouring the divine nature within ourselves and depending of your invocation, you are adding specific energy keyed to your intent to the circle or working.

I always do an invocation of the Universal. The main reasons for invoking the Universal are that by invoking the universal, you are ensuring that your intent for the working will not interfere with the universal order of things. It shows that you have respect for the natural order and that you consider consequences of doing a working Remember, this is a mindset. This is not a universal law. By using the Universal in circle, we alert our subconscious to the fact that what we are doing must be in harmony with nature, and if it is not, then the magick won't work.

The invocation of the deity is similar to invoking the quarters. The following description applies when invoking a generic Goddess and God, although you can substitute your deity as you choose to. Stand at the Altar, or in the centre of the circle. Visualise the Goddess, see her in your mind's eye, feel the feelings that she evokes from you, visualise her coming closer and entering you as you say the invocation. Once you have invoked the Goddess, light the Goddess candle, and invoke the God in the same way.

Below are generic God and Goddess invocations, which I normally use:
Goddess
    Great Goddess,
    I invite you into this sacred space
    You, who are the mother of all
    The ultimate feminine
    Bring into this circle your love and nurturing
    Hail and Welcome

God
    Great God,
    I invite you into this sacred space
    You, who are the father of all
    The ultimate masculine
    Bring into this circle your love and nurturing
    Hail and Welcome

Universal calling
    Great Universal Spirit
    That is the beginning and the end
    The male & female
    The known and unknown
    The seen and unseen
    The creative source of all
    We welcome you to this sacred space to bless and guide us
    Hail and welcome

THE WORKING

This is the part of the ritual where the working is done. This is where you will raise energy, create the spell or do a meditation or pathworking. During the seasonal celebration, this can be a reading or poetry done to commemorate the Sabbat. In group rituals, it is usually the High Priestess that does the final direction of energy towards the goal, although this can be changed to suit your circumstances. Any excess energy is usually grounded into the earth to assist with healing of the planet.

CLOSING DOWN THE RITUAL

The closing down of the ritual, involves thanking and dismissing the elements, deity and finally the circle. The order that you use when you dismiss depends on the order that you invoked in, thus I devoke the deity by saying something like
'God/ Goddess, I thank you for you participation in this ritual. Hail and farewell'

Then the quarters are devoked, and finally the circle is taken down. To take down the circle, walk around the circle with your athame extended, like when you cast the circle, but in the opposite direction that you cast in. Then say something like,
'I take down this circle, returning all the energies to the earth'
Repeat this until you have completed the circle and say 'So mote it be'

ROLES IN RITUAL

Traditionally, a circle has a High Priest (HP) and a High Priestess (HPS). The feminine invocations are done by the High Priestess, and the masculine invocations by the High Priest. They are also, traditionally, the people who represent deity, thus if your deity isn't neatly binary, neither is your High Priest and High Priestess. For ease of language, I use the term clergy. The Clergy can be a single person who writes runs and directs the ritual, but it can also be a pair or a group, depending on how you set the ritual up.

Where the clergy write and run the ritual, they are the ones in charge of saying who goes where (like a director of a play) especially in working groups and covens, the members may invoke the quarters, cast the circle, raising energy or any other rites performed in the ritual. You can also have a clergy person doing both the High Priest and High Priestess roles, or split it amongst a pair (for binary deities) or a group of three (where you use masculine, feminine and non-binary divine). It should be noted that when doing a ritual for a group it is helpful to have a single person or a pair who directs and controls the rituals and its energies.

LAYING OUT OF YOUR CIRCLE

The circle should be big for you to move around in comfortable. For a single person a circle with a six-foot diameter should be sufficient. If at all possible, ritual should be done outside, so that one can commune with nature while communing with deity.

For groups, it is important to make sure that the circle is big enough for the working that you are planning. If you are going to raise energy with a spiral dance, for instance, the circle must be big enough to accommodate it.

DEMARCATE CIRCLE: OUTSIDE OF CIRCLE & QUARTERS

The first step is to demarcate your circle, I've commonly used stones for this. The stones will absorb some of the energy that is present in the circle, and if you keep those stones aside, and use them specifically for demarcating the circle, they will continue to absorb energy and they become part of what makes your circle stronger each time. One of the easiest ways to demarcate a circle is as follows:

CHOOSE A CENTRE

Visualise where you think your circle should go and choose a point that is approximately centre. Place a rock at this point.

FIND NORTH

Using a compass find North. The other way of finding a direction is to see the direction that the sun is setting, this is West. The direction where the sun rises from is East.

MEASURE DISTANCE TO EDGE OF CIRCLE

Stand and the centre of the circle and measure to the end of the circle, at your first quarter. Place a rock at this quarter.

DEMARCATE QUARTERS

Go back to the centre and measure out the rest of the quarters placing a rock at each.

DEMARCATE REST OF CIRCLE

Then go back to the centre and measure out points between the quarters. Depending on the size of the circle, mark between one and three points between the quarters. This will ensure that the circle is round.

SET UP ALTAR

Choose where you want your altar to be and place it there. Then set up the altar with all the tools on it. Place all other items that will be required for the ritual in their places in the circle. For example, place the quarter candles at the quarters, the cauldron in the middle (if you are going to be using one) etc.

Light the incense or coals allow the incense to burn. Do not light any candles, as you do not want to leave an open flame unattended.

SWEEP WITH BESOM

Using the besom, sweep the circle in the direction that you would cast the circle namely deosil. As you sweep the circle (without the bristles touching the ground), visualise all the resident energy being swept away and the circle becoming sacred space. When you are satisfied that you have cleared the circle of all energy, you can stop. Place the besom either at the altar, or the entrance to the circle.

GUESTS

If you are brining other people into the circle, either as guests or active participants, it is a good idea to cleanse them as well. This is done by 'smudging' and 'anointing'.

Smudging means that you use the elements of fire and air to cleanse the person. Light incense (an incense stick works the best for this) and then, using a feather or your hand, sweep the incense smoke towards the person. This is usually done from head to toe on the front of the person, and the person from foot to head of the back of the person. There is not specific reason for this technique, other than it is the most practical when smudging a large group. The smoke of the incense cleanses the person's aura as well as the smell alerts their subconscious to the purpose of the ritual, allowing the person to mentally prepare for the ritual.

Anointing means that you place specially made oil onto the forehead of a person to consecrate that person with the magickal qualities of that oil. The anointing oil is usually something that dispels negativity and increases psychicism. To anoint someone, take a vial of oil (usually a mixture matched to your intent), place some oil on the tip of your finger, and place the oil in the centre of the person's forehead. When doing this some people just trace a circle, others do the sign of the Goddess and still others draw a Pentagram, what you do is up to you, but remember, use only a small amount of oil, the last thing you need is to blind your guests will oil flowing in their eyes!

In some circles, usually only in coven work, the High Priest or High Priestess will only allow guests in after they have correctly answered the challenge. This is done by pointing the Athame at the person and asking 'What do you bring to sacred space?' (or something similar), and the correct answer should be 'Perfect Love and Perfect Trust' (or something similar).

When working with others, you can do one of three things. One, allow them into the circle before you cast or, two, have them wait outside the circle until the casting is done and then let them in through a portal, which is then closed behind them, or three, not allow them into the sacred space, but allow them to sit on the outskirts of the circle. Do what feels comfortable for you.

LIBATION

The cakes and ale section for the ritual has various purposes depending on when it occurs in the ritual, and the people in the ritual. The cakes and ale can be to revive the participants after raising energy and performing magick, it can be to give everyone a chance to socialise and grow closer in circle; it can be used to prepare the participants for the raising of energy or to allow the participants to relax near the end of the ritual.

Cakes and ale entails blessing the ale, fruit juice or wine and thank the deity, then bless the cakes, biscuits, bread or fruit. The plate and cup (usually the chalice) gets passed around while people give the cake they say, 'may you never hunger', and when they pass the ale they say, 'may you never thirst'.

When doing the Cakes and ale, one does not have to use actual cakes and ale. At many a handfasting I have seen strawberries and champagne shared, which has worked quite well for the occasion. The rule of thumb for what to use is to make sure everyone is catered for, if you are serving wine or actual ale, make sure that you have fruit juice for those people who don't drink alcohol.

CIRCLE ETIQUETTE

Some customs of Pagan ceremonies are not evident that are not Pagan, and to those who have never entered a Pagan circle. The circle is the space where the ceremony will be held in, and in Pagan terms, the circle can be seen as a temporary church and thus, certain rules of conduct apply. This is done to ensure that everyone within the circle has peace of mind, and to facilitate a joyous and harmonious celebration.

The Wiccan law that states *"an' it harm none, do what ye will"* will be abided to in and outside of the circle.

During the ceremony, the High Priestess and High Priest have absolute authority. Once the ceremony has started, no one may leave, or enter without their express permission, and this will only be given under exceptional circumstances. (Therefore, go to the bathroom beforehand!)

Be Punctual – The circle will start at the set time and anyone not in circle; will not be allowed in afterwards.

If you are drunk, stoned, drugged or on very strong prescription medication, you don't belong in Circle. Excuse yourself and leave. Otherwise, the High Priestess or High Priest may have to escort you out.

No smoking, eating or drinking will be allowed in circle, unless deigned by the High Priestess or the High Priest. Do not bring food, drink or sweets into sacred space (the circle) for private consumption during ritual.

Focus on the ceremony that is taking place, your behaviour should reflect your respect for your deity and those around you. Inappropriate talking, joking, laughing in small groups during the ritual are considered extremely rude and break the concentration and continuity of the ceremony.

The circle is sacred, and thus it will be required for all to be barefoot while in circle.

No one will be allowed skyclad (naked) in the circle unless with the express permission of the High Priest and High Priestess.

Reserve all question for before or after the ritual. The High Priest and High Priestess will be willing to answer any questions that you may have.

Pagan ceremonies are not necessarily solemn affairs, have fun and enjoy the experience.

Section 6:
Divination

13. DIVINATION

Divination is the art of being able to predict the future, or to be able to tell information about a person or event through unconventional means. There are many different forms of divination, and many different tools that can be used. This book will cover some of the more common forms of divination, but it is up to you to find the type of divination that suits you. Some people choose a form of divination as stick to it for their whole lives, whereas some people move through the different types in stages as they change, they learn a new divination tool. Some people never do divination, because they just don't have the knack for it, and still some don't out of principle. I think everyone should try at least two forms of divination, even if it is just once.

COMMON SPREADS

There are a few common spreads that can be used for both Tarot cards, other types of divination cards, and runes. A spread is a way of organising and asking a question. You have specific areas of the spread (positions) that represent specific things (for example, the past, the present, the future etc.), and you then place the cards in those specific positions. Remember, the position as well as the meaning of the card need to be taken into consideration when doing a reading.

A SIMPLE THREE CARD SPREAD

When using rune or a card in a spread, you would leave all the runes in your bag, set out the cloth on a table or floor. At this stage you should ask Odin to give you wisdom and insight so you will get a true reading. Now once this is done ask your question while shaking the bag of runes, when you feel ready take out the first of three runes and place them down one by one in a row on your cloth as shown.

If you are doing a card reading, shuffle the cards while asking the question and ask your chosen deity to give you wisdom and insight into the cards you are about to read. Then take 3 cards out of the deck and lay them down as follows:

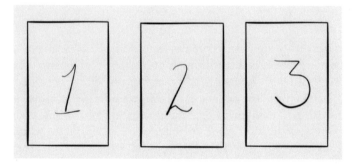

This is the triple rune/card reading, it is read from left to right and can be read as one concise answer; or past, present, future, it is up to you.

ELEMENTAL CROSS

Let's look at the Elemental cross, shake the runes as you did before but now get 5 runes out of your bag, or shuffle the cards and choose 5 cards (without looking at what cards they are). Place them down in the shown order.

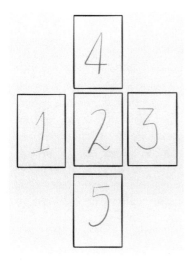

1. Signifies the past.
2. Signifies the present.
3. Signifies the future.
4. Indicates the kind of help the querent can expect.
5. Indicates aspects that cannot be changed at this time and must be accepted.

SEVEN CARD TYR SPREAD

This is a seven-card spread named after the rune TYR.

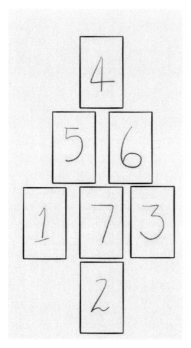

With this spread the first four runes/cards are laid out as numbered to form a cross. Then the runes left in the bag are shaken again and 3 more runes are taken and placed in the 5, 6, and 7 to form TYR.

1. The origin of the question, feelings and reason.
2. Best possible outcome.
3. Obstacles that might block the outcome.
4. What is likely to cause failure.
5. Past influences.
6. Present influences.
7. Future influences that affect the outcome.

RUNES

The runes date as far back as 150AD. No one can pinpoint where the runes first came from, only that there is much evidence that the early Celtic and Germanic tribes used them extensively. This seems to be their first form of writing that they used, but because most people of the day could not read or write, the runes were seen as mystical and had great power. In the past 2,000 years very little has changed in the way the runes are read, the way the runes are cast have changed from rune caster to rune caster.

Today there are many different sets of runes available, even rune cards. You can find runes made of plastic, wood, gold, silver, clay and card. I myself have over the years used and owned many of these sets, but I always find myself going back to the set I made myself because they just feel right.

You can always buy a readymade set from a shop, but I feel that it would be a worthwhile and a good learning exercise to attempt to make your own. By making your own rune set you will be learning the meanings of the runes, you will also be creating a very powerful link between your rune set and yourself, by adding some of your life force to them, and if you are anything like me, you could end up cutting a finger or two and end up blessing your new set with some blood. I do not go out of my way to cut myself, I'm just clumsy.

The traditional material for making the runes is Oak, ash or yew, but I will use any fruit-bearing tree, my best set is made out of peach tree. Before you go cutting down all your trees to find a straight branch, you should go and have a look at the trees around your home and ask them to give you a branch. When you do find a branch to suit your needs; which could take a few days, you must always give thanks to the tree and give it a gift; which could be anything that feels right. Now that you have your branch, you must take of the bark and then let the peace of wood dry out inside. This should take about 2 to 3 weeks if it's dry and longer if the weather is wet. When the branch is dry cut it up into 30 pieces of equal size. You will only need 25 but keep some for spare as mistakes do happen from time to time. The shape of the runes does not make a difference as long as the runes are uniform and you are happy with them.

Now comes the fun part, drawing the runes. You can paint, carve or burn on the runes. By carving the runes and painting them after can give you an effective finish. While carving the runes look up their meanings, this will help you to learn them and place the right energy into them. Once you have completed your rune set you need a bag to carry them in and a cloth to cast them on. Your bag should be made of any natural cloth like cotton, leather or silk it should also be black to keep any unwanted energy away from your runes. Your cloth for casting can be any natural martial and any colour you like, but you should keep it with your runes at all times.

Before using your new runes they should be consecrated and blessed in a simple ritual. You can do this with the runes, bag and cloth by cleansing them with coarse salt and incense. As you pass them through the salt and incense you can recite something like this:

> With salt and smoke I remove all that is not wanted
> All that is not needed,
> All negative energy I remove from these my tools
> So they will aid me well and guide me true
> Odin, lord of the runes
> Bless my tools
> Grant me the wisdom and insight
> To see what lies ahead
> And may they never lead me astray.

CASTING THE RUNES

There are many ways of casting the runes. About the oldest way known today is to blow on the runes while asking a question and then to cast them on to your cloth, in much the same way the African sangoma casts the bones. The rune master would read the runes by the lay of them, what rune is next to what, how far away are the runes lying away from the centre and so on. You can read the runes like you would with the tarot by using pre-set spreads.

Runes are very powerful tools, which we still can use today for divination and in workings, but a word of warning: they need to be respected and used with care, as they can be used both positively and negatively.

DIVINATORY MEANINGS OF THE RUNES

There are a couple of different runic alphabets in use today; we will be using the Futhark, which is the most commonly used and has 24 characters.

 Feoh: Upright: Money, success, great wealth, freedom
Reversed: Bankruptcy, loss of personal esteem, failure, and no control.

 Ur: Upright: Good fortune, advancement in career, good health.
Reversed: Missed chances, negative influences, bad luck, and bad health.

 Thorn: Upright: Protection, an important decision, good news from afar, unexpected luck.
Reversed: Beware, making any hasty decisions, bad news.

 As: Upright: Wisdom or wise counsel from an elderly person or knowledgeable person, learning and communication.
Reversed: A elderly person who causes problems, incorrect advice from a spiteful source, rumours and lies.

 Rad: Upright: Travel, a spiritual journey, movement, holiday that brings joy, moving between worlds.
Reversed: A bad or difficult journey, delays, a visit to sick relative or friend in trouble.

 Cen: Upright: Spiritual enlightenment, artistic creativity, writing, guidance from divine sources, to know.
Reversed: Loss of prestige, social standing and material possessions, loss of divine guidance, to be at a loss.

Gyfu: Upright: A gift which is a symbol of shared love, a binding relationship.

Wyn: Upright: Joy and happiness, the transforming of life for the better.
Reversed: Unhappiness, grief, loss of love and affection.

Hagel: Upright: A delay in plans, set back in work.
Reversed: Disasters caused by natural forces or anything not in human control, delays.

Nyd: Upright: Forces of fate are at work, caution is needed, resist greed.
Reversed: Hasty action leading to failure, stop or proceed with care.

Is: Upright: The ending of activity, cooling of a relationship, disagreements with close friends.

Ger: Upright: Happiness, movement, building, harvest, hard work paying off, end of stillness.

Eoh: Upright: News of a death, past problems, the unknown, assistance from an old acquaintance or friend.

Peorth: Upright: Hidden knowledge, unexpected gains, a secret gift or love, a home of warmth and love, a spirit guide. Reversed: Secrets revealed that causes harm, unpleasant surprises, non-beneficial things coming to notice, hidden illness.

Eolh: Upright: Banishment of negative influences, protection, a new and good influences, new career or friendship.
Reversed: A warning of attack that could lead to material loss, death, radical change, deception.

Sigil: Upright: Success, health, wise-direction, failure of all opposition, limitless energy, proceed unchanged.

Tyr: Upright: Success by self-sacrifice, success in legal matters, sexual relationship.
Reversed: Unrequited love, marital problems, giving up, emotional problems, sexual problems.

Beorc Upright: New beginnings of all kinds, birth of a child or idea, jump into action without delay with anything new, marriage, growth.
Reversed: Lack of growth, warning of problems, stagnation in relationships, failure in business.

Ehwaz: Upright: A journey that could lead to moving house, job changes, marriage, alteration in lifestyle, fruitful partnerships.
Reversed: Restlessness, travel difficulties, breaking of relationships, discovery of false friends, make no major changes at this time.

Man: Upright: Harmony with one's surroundings, a balanced frame of mind, good judgement, contact with the outside world.

Reversed: Self-imposed isolation, obstruction of plans, warning of enemies, individual's negative attitudes.

Lagu: Upright: Growth through education, spiritual teaching, fertile imagination, sympathy of others, inspiration and intuition.

Reversed: Confusion, delusion, muddled thinking, bad judgement, failed love affairs.

Ing: Upright: Realization of a dream, beneficial life-changing events, being free from worries and completion of a stage.

Dag: Upright: Prosperity, new day dawning, demolition of barriers, change of mind and change of the better.

Odal: Upright: Safety and protection, money not immediately available, spiritual skills from ones past, good out-come with property.

Reversed: Over-stretching of resources, delays, lack of attention to detail, legal problems with property and being self-reliant.

THE TAROT

The tarot is a set of cards that forms the basis of the current playing cards today. The tarot cards are reported to have started in antiquity when paganism was dying out and witches were being persecuted. It is said to have been a way for the gypsies to represent their knowledge to pass to the next generation without being found out, because upon questioning, the gypsy would say it is a card game. How accurate this origin is, is questionable, but it seems to be the most widely accepted.

Then in 1911, AE Waite wrote a book called The Pictorial key to the Tarot, which firmly placed him as the father of tarot. This was done in collaboration with PC Smith who illustrated the cards. This was published by the Rider Publishing house and since then, the Rider- Waite tarot has been the foundation for many tarot decks available.

Tarot cards are more than just a divinatory system. The tarot can be used in workings and spells to signify what the card represents. The images on the tarot cards are linked to our subconscious and collective unconscious and are therefore representative of the archetypes.

The tarot consists of two parts, also known as arcane (which means), the major/greater arcane, and the Minor arcane. When you begin with the tarot, it is best to start with just the major arcane (included below) until you get to know these well, before moving onto the lesser arcane.

NUMEROLOGY

Numerology involves telling and foretelling using numbers based on your name or your birth date. There are different types of numbers that can be used, for different purposes.

DESTINY NUMBER

From your destiny number, you can divine all the talent and potential that you have available to you during this lifetime. To work out your destiny number you use your full name, if you've changed your name, you can change your destiny.

Use the table below to associate numbers to letters in your name:

1	2	3	4	5	6	7	8	9
A	B	C	D	E	F	G	H	I
J	K	L	M	N	O	P	Q	R
S	T	U	V	W	X	Y	Z	

So for example, if you use the name

Leo Green
3+5+6+7+9+5+5+5 = 45
4+5 = 9

Therefore, this Destiny number is 9.

LIFE PATH

The Life Path is determined by the number that you get to when reducing your birth date to a single digit and shows the traits and talents that you were born with and the probable journey you will take during your lifetime.

For example:

A birth date of the 19th August 1979, also written as the 19/ 08/ 1979.
1+9 + 8 + 1+ 9 + 7 + 9 = 44
4+4 = 8
This Life path number is 8.

PERSONALITY NUMBER

Your personality number shows your personality. This is sometimes seen as being your public face that you show the world, thus your personality number can differ greatly from your Life Path, Destiny and Soul Numbers. To work out your personality number, first we take all the vowels out of your name. So, Leo Green becomes:

LGRN

Then, Use the table below to associate numbers to consonants in your name:

1	2	3	4	5	6	7	8	9
	B	C	D		F	G	H	
J	K	L	M	N		P	Q	R
S	T		V	W	X	Y	Z	

LGRN
3+7+9+5 = 24
2 + 4 = 6
The Personality Number is 6

SOUL NUMBER

Your Soul Number represents the number that shows your soul, who you are on the inside, and what you want and value most in life. This may be very different from what your Life Path number (that represents who you are from birth) or your Destiny number (that represents your potential). For your soul number, you use only the vowels of you name, (so these are the ones you left out for your Personality number). So, Leo Green becomes:

EOEE

1	2	3	4	5	6	7	8	9
A				E				I
					O			
		U						

E O E E
5+6+5+5 = 21
2+1 = 3
Thus, their Soul number is 3.

THE MEANING OF THE NUMBERS

ONE

Planet: Sun
Astrological sign: Aries, Capricorn
Key word: Individuality

One is very egocentric, quite often being somewhat of a loner.

Ones are very independent, thus as a destiny number, one is someone who can take risks, have original ideas, makes things happen and are often entrepreneurs. They have motivation, enthusiasm, creativity and inspiration. They are ambitious and determined and are often very self-confident. They can be egotistical, self-absorbed, dominant, impatient and sometimes act too hastily to ensure they don't miss out on an opportunity. Their aggression and ambition is often interpreted as hostility and selfishness. Ones need to learn to be patient, and tolerant of other people's ideas. They also need to learn about the value of good timing, and tact.

In terms of a life path number one, you are motivated by a need for freedom, independence (emotional and financial) and personal attainment. You have a potential to be great leaders, but they can fail at teamwork and cooperation.

As a personality, a one likes to portray themselves to others as a great leader or grand master. They desire to be admired for their courage, daring and creative ideas. They want others to perceive them as infallible. Although you may feel that they are simply being assertive or taking charge, others may perceive them as aggressive, arrogant and even hostile.

For one as a soul number, people with a number one desire to be the best in all areas of their life, they want to be the first in all things to get them to stand out in a crowd. More than anything the almost childish soul number one secretly desires unconditional approval from others.

TWO

Planet: Moon
Astrological sign: Taurus, Aquarius
Key Word: Compromise

Two is very co-operative, emotive, and has a great deal of feeling. This number is associated with relationships in general.

As a destiny number, two is a number of mediation, peacemaking and compromise. This often leads them to professions as team leads, facilitators and mediators. They tend to have many friends because of their diplomacy and courtesy. However erratic behaviours, drama queens and overt displays of physical affection upset them.

Some twos can be shy and eager to please, but they need to learn to not allow others to take advantage of them.

Those following a two life path, have an inherent sense of morality and fairness, and tend to only see the best in others. They tend to be indecisive as they can clearly see both sides of any conundrum or argument. They often make judges, mediators, lawyers, counsellors or social workers because they have an incredible talent for resolving disputes.

Number twos function best in nine to five jobs where the routine is the same every day and are the type to keep everything that they have owned since birth in the attic or basement. They are also very sentimental and nostalgic, many of them collect antiques and photographs of loved ones. Because of the need to bring harmony to group situations it is very important for number twos to get out and socialize.

For a number two personality number, twos like to portray themselves to others as one who is beyond any negative emotions such as jealousy or hate. It is important for them to look popular and well loved by others. However this can lead to being treated like a doormat.

Individuals with this number have a deep desire to always be right, it is their desire for respect that leads them to be so difficult sometimes. Soul number twos can benefit from developing an accepting rather than autocratic approach when dealing with other people.

THREE

Planet: Jupiter
Astrological Sign: Gemini, Pisces
Keyword: Attention

Three is educated, wise, and happy. The acquisition or expenditure of money often features prominently in the number. Money will come and go easily when three is significant.

Those born with Number 3 as their destiny number excel at all persuasive talents. These include writing, speaking, singing, acting, litigating, and teaching selling, designing and composing music. An often unexploited talent of a number three is their natural ability to uplift others with their words and ideas.

Sometimes Number threes have a tendency to be shallow or superficial. They are best to save their dramatic talents for the stage, podium or silver screen. Followers of Life Path number three are effervescent personalities whose journey often leads to artistic acclaim or social popularity. Number threes are entertainers of the world and most of them are truly gifted musicians, writers, actors, dancers, public speakers and politicians.

A number three is not fulfilled until there has been some public acknowledgement of his or her unique talent but they are also known for their understanding of human nature as well as their ability to listen to others and truly comprehend their emotional needs.

The number threes can be stubborn and play to win, irrespective of the cost of success, but if they do fail they are more resilient than others. These failures are usually in the financial or romantic areas, because their spontaneity can cause them to make bad decisions. However a number three is usually quite humble and very capable of being honest with themselves about their mistakes.

Threes usually present themselves as having great talents, even if they don't. They tend to crave attention, and this can lead to bad behaviour which can make then seem manipulative and shallow to others.

Threes great desire is to be beautiful. In childhood they are usually the ugly ducklings and even though many of them do grow into swans, they still often feel that there is something wrong with their appearance. Soul Number threes may resort to plastic surgery, to correct what they see as flaws or to stop the aging process.

FOUR

Planet: Mars
Astrological Sign: Cancer
Key Word: Organisation

Four is forceful and dominating in an attempt to control the tension that is inherent in this number. It also has a great deal of stability and is therefore a good number when attempting to build foundations. When four is prominent, quite often people will need to overcome obstacles before they will be able to reach their highest potential.

People with a destiny number four thrive best in a corporate environment. Their unique skills are administration, project management and all kinds of organization. Number fours also make surgeons, architects, engineers, musicians and teachers. They work well with their hands and have an innate understanding of structure, design and rhythm.

Unfortunately, Number fours rarely get anything handed to them, but are amply rewarded for their efforts. Hard work and determination are the keys to success for a number four. Number fours can however be rigid or dogmatic in their thinking. They are black and white thinkers with strong likes and dislikes, which needs to be overcome by learning tolerance, patience and acceptance.

Those following the Life Path of a number 4 often end up becoming the pillars of the community. These individuals are hardworking, practical and trustworthy. They have the practical skills to bring dreams of others into reality. However they often demand too much both of themselves and others, which leads them to be seen as either martyrs or tyrants. The will power and stubbornness can be misinterpreted as greed and selfishness, which baffles the number four who usually has the best intentions. Number fours can get upset if their routines are tampered with, and they do not respond to criticism well. Number fours are associated with the earth element so they can have a very grounding influence on others. They can also be so over focused on the tasks at hand that they miss big opportunities that come their way.

People following the number 4 life path are often learning lessons about letting go of emotional insecurity and to develop some flexibility and tolerance of others.

People with a personality number of four present themselves as a pillar of the community, the rock that other people can come to for advice solace and help. They make yourself indispensable to others by running their schedules for them, organizing their affairs and finding solutions to their problems. However behind this mask of confidence lies a very insecure individual who fears rejection.

The four soul number craves emotional and financial security. As a result they can be clingy, possessive and controlling of their loved ones. Their fear of taking risks can also cause them to be stuck, especially when it comes to academics and career. Number fours tend to stick to what they know works and react with hostility to any suggestion about change. Developing the confidence to handle anything that comes their way is the best way for number fours to overcome their insecurity.

FIVE

Planet: Mercury
Astrological Sign: Leo
Key Word: Restlessness

It is very communicative and witty on a light level. Because this number deals with the concept of communication, on a negative level deception can also be involved, so it is always best to double check for the facts.

People born with a destiny number of five are usually born with many talents and abilities. They often awe others with their competence in all areas of life. These masters of flexibility and change are also great innovators and inventors. Their quick wit and charm often makes them very popular socially. Fives tend to bore easily so they very seldom stay in one career for long, but they need to learn to follow through and finish one thing before starting another.

Those travelling the number five Life Path are adventurous and highly inquisitive individuals who consider hands on experience to be the best teacher in life. Many of them are deeply intelligent, philosophical and spiritually minded. They love to theorize about the nature of existence and they loathe routine and daily chores. They are often excellent at initiating many projects, but rarely finish any of them. Most number fives are terrible at self-care and housework, preferring instead to follow their whims and impulses. For this reason, they do not thrive well in office environments.

At some point in their life, a number 5 experiences some kind of spiritual or emotional awakening that causes them to trade in a standard career for a self-made profession such as an artist, investigator or journalist. Number fives lack the discipline or desire to follow one path and hate to make plans and prefer to live in the present, which may be disastrous for their financial security. Their happy-go-lucky attitudes demonstrate an incredible faith that the universe will take care of them. The number 5's lack of commitment also extends to personal relationships. They tend to be very self-absorbed and unaware of the effect of their actions on other people.

The person that has a five as a personality number shows themselves as a freedom loving spirit who is unrestrained by the usual responsibilities. They like to present themselves to others as a seeker of spiritual truth as well as an individual who can make friends in any situation. Sometimes their holier than thou attitude seems patronizing or contemptuous to people that they meet.

Soul Number fives desire freedom more than anything else in their lives. They are somewhat claustrophobic and feel very confined by office jobs and routines. To avoid apathy and depression, number fives should seek out careers that involve a great deal of travel or a flexible time schedule. They function best as the owners of their own business or as entrepreneurs. Developing a regimen of spiritual study also greatly assists fives as that helps them quell their restlessness and develop a sense of inner peace.

SIX

Planet: Venus
Astrological sign: Virgo
Keyword: Family

Six is a pleasant, harmonious number that governs the arts and music. Tact and diplomacy figure prominently with this number, so relationships will be of paramount importance. Many opportunities for success come to the individuals who this number has touched.

With is a destiny number of six, they are born diplomats who can restore balance to any disharmonious situation. These exceptional individuals are born with an innate talent of uplifting the spirits of others, especially during hard times. Some of them do this through service and others accomplish this through art, music or writing. Whether they are conscious of it or not, their destiny is often to restore faith in hearts that are broken. Number 6's are very concerned with family and children, and many of them feel unfulfilled in life if they don't get the chance to raise a family. People who are a number six have a lot to offer in terms of parenting as no other number understands the mind of a child better.

Number 6's can sabotage their success by being too demanding of themselves. Many of them have bad childhoods that cause them to grow up with a severe inner critic that constantly tells them that they are not good enough, and they need to learn to be as loving, caring and respectful of themselves as they are to others.

Those following the number 6 Life Path are usually people-pleasers that have a great need to feel indispensable to others. These self-less individuals believe that they should share the burdens of others as they proceed on their life's journey. They are usually mature souls who are not afraid to assume responsibility or take charge of difficult situations. Number sixes usually feel a spiritual obligation to help others and do so by constantly displaying kindness, tenderness and compassion to all that they meet.

Number sixes are also domestic creatures whose actions are often motivated by a love of children and family. It is rare for a number six to have money problems, unless the cause is assisting someone who is less fortunate. They usually earn the unqualified respect of family and friends because of their willingness to carry more than their share. Number sixes have a tendency to co-dependency.

With a personality number six, they need to fit in with the societal norm. Number 6's like to be perceived as hard-working, ethical individuals who value their families above all. It is a six that is most likely to lose his or her sense of identity, and they need to have a partner and a family to feel complete and fulfilled.

Soul Number 6's desire justice at all costs. These proactive individuals consider themselves to be agents of karma and often work behind the scenes to punish the undeserving and reward those who they consider to be underdogs. They are also perfectionists on many levels and often make unrealistic demands on themselves and others in their never ending quest to balance the score. To mitigate a tendency to resent all authority or judge a book by its cover, sixes need to learn a tolerance and acceptance of others who do not share their opinions or moral standards.

151

SEVEN

Planet: Neptune
Astrological Sign: Libra
Key word: Spirituality

Seven is a very spiritual number that is not limited by the constraints of the physical world. This is the number of mystics, visionaries, and seers. Because this number is associated with idealism, depression can easily manifest itself when our expectations of others and our goals are not met. This number has many surreal, or unreal, qualities to it.

Those born with a number seven Destiny number tend to be thoughtful introverts who treasure privacy and seclusion. Sevens can appear to be eccentric, cold and withdrawn to others, and they believe in saying as little as possible. Their best way to express emotion is to write their feelings down on paper and show it to others.

Those embarking on number seven life path are affectionate, peace-loving individuals who prefer rationality to inspiration. Number sevens are perfectionists who prefer silence to music, noise and crowds. They are methodical and thorough analysts who believe that if you can't do a job right, don't do it at all. Suspicious 7's do not make friends easily. They often appear very reserved and aloof to others and many find it takes some time to even get up the nerve to approach them. Once a seven does make a friend, however, it is usually for life. Although they are sceptical and analytical creatures, sevens rely on their gut instincts more than they rely on statistics, public opinion polls or advice from others and they dislike being manipulated.

The shadow side of a 7 is a tendency to become pessimistic, overly logical, quarrelsome and pessimistic.

Those with a personality number of seven prefer others to perceive them as mystical or wise creatures that may possess secret knowledge. For this reason they tend to say little in social situations and display as little emotion as possible. Many of them are secretive introverts who prefer the company of a good book to a human being. Behind this mask of moral superiority however often lies a powerful fear of rejection. They are afraid of being humiliated or rejected if they should bare their wild thoughts and dreams to another individual.

The seven soul numbers desire unconditional love. Many of them come from abusive or addicted families, so often they succumb to addiction or co dependences with toxic partners. Sevens are often motivated by the urge to love others without conditions, as they have always desired the same for themselves. Unfortunately their kindness is not always rewarded, as they tend to choose emotionally unavailable, mentally ill or otherwise difficult partners. Individuals following this difficult soul path often learn several hard lessons about letting go of bad relationships.

EIGHT

Planet: Saturn
Astrological sign: Scorpio
Keyword: Materialism

Eight is a solid and very stable number that has many limitations that must be transcended. Those individuals who have this number prominent in their life usually must learn by experience.

Those born with the Destiny number eight are fated to make money during their lifetime. They have the potential for considerable achievement in business or other powerful positions, however many of them are simply born into wealthy families. Number 8's are also very practical and seem to have a knack for building and accumulating wealth. A downside to this is that sometimes their desire to acquire more money becomes a burning desire that causes them to ignore family, friends and social life. Although it seems that Number eights have it easy, much of their success is due to their sound judgement when it comes to money and commercial matters. Eights are also excellent judges of character and do not suffer fools gladly.

Followers of the number 8 Life Path are naturally lucky individuals whose soul purpose is to acquire material wealth. People on this path have relatively little time for dreams and visions, as they are busy applying their prodigal organizational abilities to the real world. Number 8s are usually confident, charismatic individuals who are adept at spotting trends and opportunities. Usually their life purpose is learning to manipulate money and power without becoming corrupted in the process. These social climbers will go to great lengths to meet the right person at the right time. Even if an eight is from an unprivileged background, he or she will go to a lot of trouble to be seen at the right parties, wearing the right clothes and hobnobbing with the real players in the room. People who boast a rags to riches history often are number eights. Courageous number 8's also have an incredible capacity to not sweat the small stuff and often beat out their competitors simply through sheer endurance or fortitude. Sometimes the pursuit of riches becomes more important than personal relationships.

The personalities of number eights believe in faking it 'til they make it. They love to appear powerful to others, so even if they don't have a dime in their pocket they will often project a charisma and confidence that is unrivalled by any other person in the room. Resourceful eights also know exactly how to flatter and compliment others so that they can get ahead in life. Some people, however, may interpret the manipulations of an eight to be dishonest, shallow and materialistic.

Soul Number eights are practical creatures that value success above all else. Although they can appear selfish and materialistic to others, their actual desire (at least in the beginning) is to create a more prosperous future for their family, friends and community. Eights are usually generous and philanthropic individuals who don't feel that they deserve love unless they offer others a gift. Often they need to learn that aside from acquiring great wealth, there are simpler routes to happiness.

NINE

Planet: Uranus
Astrological sign: Sagittarius
Keyword: Eccentric

Nine is very eccentric and unusual in nature. Where this number is prominent invention and ingenuity are very important elements to any given situation.

Number nine's destiny often lies within the sphere of humanitarian causes. Nines are not very career driven and are born with an innate understanding of human nature. These kind, considerate and compassionate individuals are often also blessed with literary or artistic gifts as well. However, as many of them are so driven to help the world and solve humanity's problems, they don't get around to expressing their artistic talents until very late in life. Nines are idealists who believe the most valuable tool for change is to put wisdom into practice. Some nines take their idealism to the point that they are always bitter and disappointed by others' reaction to their philanthropic works. In order to live up to his or her highest potential, a nine must take care not to be carried away by principles as this can lead to aloofness and pride.

Those on the number 9 Life path are destined to travel a humanitarian path. These sophisticated individual are very selfless souls and are often patient, trustworthy and honourable from the very beginning to the end of their life. Their moral rectitude, compassion and generosity often identify them. Very few nines are interested in material gain, they believe rather that they will be rewarded after life, rather than in this one.

Number 9's have winning smiles and make friends very easily. They are great listeners and many of them can make others feel better just with a simple pat on the hand. Personal relationships often seem toxic to sophisticated number nines who are turned off by the drama, possessiveness and terminal uniqueness that is associated with the ideal of a soul mate. Nines' eccentricity causes others to treat them like village idiot. Sometimes nine's lofty ideals are presented in a manner that others find absurd, spacey or hilarious. Part of a nine's life path to express spiritual principles through actions, rather than through preaching or converting.

The personality number nine goes to a great deal of trouble to convince others that they are creative or intellectual. The face they present to others is often very eccentric or eclectic as most of them suffer from a bad case of terminal uniqueness. Still others are often very touched by their genuine concern. Behind their lofty airs and random acts of kindness is usually a huge ego that is craving the respect of others.

Those born with a Soul Number 9 have a great desire to transcend all karma by using humour. They are also great teachers as they have a way of transforming spiritual messages and philosophies into entertainment for the masses. Most of them are gentle souls who have made it their life mission to make the world into a kinder place. Many of them are also liberal thinkers who support the right of each individual to make their own mistakes. Their motto is 'Remember to take time out to smell the flowers.'

SCRYING

Scrying involves looking into a semi reflective surface, and seeing images from another plane. Focusing on the surface is done to keep the conscious mind busy, while the subconscious mind reveals information from another plane of existence. This is also seen as a type of mediumship. This is one of the hardest forms of divination, because it takes a lot of hard work, practice and natural talent for you to use scrying as a form of divination. The types of objects that can be used for scrying are:

- A Crystal Ball – Preferable one with exclusions and that has a light behind it (preferably candle light)
- A Bowl of Water – Preferably a bowl made of glass, brass or silver
- A Bowl of water where you drip drops of ink into
- A Mirror – Preferably a round or oval mirror, backed with silver
- A Black Mirror – This is a like a normal mirror, but the mirror has been painted or stained black.
- Tea Leaves in the bottom of a cup – There are many rules about how to prepare the tea leaves, so read more about this before you try.

A common method of divination is:

Find a place that is quiet and free from distractions

Sit comfortably with the object (ball, mirror or bowl of water) in front of you

Focus on the object, still your mind and wait for the images to appear.

Speak as these images appear, and describe them, this often assists your mind into moving into a trance like state, which will assist in the divination.

Take notes, or have someone else take notes of the images that you see. You can interpret them once the session is over.

PALMISTRY

Palmistry is also known as palm-reading, chorology, hand analysis or chiromancy and involves reading the lines, markings, mounds of the hand and fingers to analyse the person and/ or predict the future of the person whose hand/s are being read. The projective hand is used to read the current and future, where the receptive hand is read to see the person's past lives, karma or hereditary traits. The following is a picture that shows some of the typical mappings of the lines on a hand:

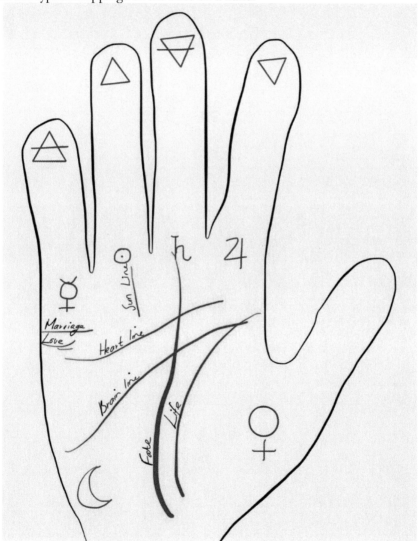

- **Heart Line**: Matter of the heart, emotional state and stability
- **Brain Line**: Intellectual matters, communication,
- **Fate Line**: This line is said to reflect you fate, and for those who don't believe in fate, said to reflect your choices and the consequences thereof.
- **Life Line**: This line is said to depict how long you will live.
- **Sun Line**: Indicate fame or scandal
- **Marriage Line**: Indicates how long you will be married for, and how many times.

WORKS CITED

Cranmer, S. R. (1999, December). *Golden Dawn Library Project*. Retrieved from The Golden Dawn FAQ: http://hermetic.com/gdlibrary/gd-faq.html

Crowley, A. (1938). *The Book of the Law*. London: Ordo Templi Orientis.

Crowley, A., Desti, M., & Waddell, L. (1998). *Magick: Liber Aba*. Newburyport: Red Wheel/Weiser Books.

Dearnaley, R. (2002). *The Influence of Aleister Crowley upon "Ye Bok of ye Art Magical"*. Retrieved from G.B. Gardner: http://geraldgardner.com/dearnaley.php

Fortune, D. (1979). *Applied Magic*. London: HarperCollins Distribution Services.

Frazer, S. J. (1922). *The Golden Bough*. New York: Macmillan Publishers.

Hodgman, C. (2010, October 21). *The war on witches*. Retrieved from History Extra: http://www.historyextra.com/witchcraft

Hoeller, S. A. (1996). *On the Trail of the Winged God, Hermes and Hermeticism Throughout the Ages*. Retrieved from The Gnosis Archive: http://gnosis.org/hermes.htm

Holzer, H. (1971). *The Truth about Witchcraft*. New York: Vintage Books.

Jacobs, R. (2013, October 30). *When Governments Go After Witches*. Retrieved from The Atlantic: http://www.theatlantic.com/international/archive/2013/10/when-governments-go-after-witches/280856/

Kapoor, M. (2015, March 19). *Witch Hunting On The Rise Across Several Indian States*. Retrieved from India Times: http://www.indiatimes.com/news/india/witch-hunting-on-the-rise-across-several-indian-states-231133.html

MacTara, D. (1999). *Monism, One Wiccan Perspective*. Retrieved from Internet Book of Shadows: http://www.sacred-texts.com/bos/bos320.htm

Newton, I. (1846). *Philosophiæ Naturalis Principia Mathematica*. New York: Daniel Adee.

Sisowath, K. (2015, Ferbuary 14). *Thoth Hermes Trismegistus and his Ancient School of Mysteries*. Retrieved from Ancient Origins: http://www.ancient-origins.net/history-famous-people/thoth-hermes-trismegistus-and-his-ancient-school-mysteries-002676?nopaging=1

Three Initiates. (1912). *The Kybalion*. Alexandria: Library of Alexandria.

ABOUT THE AUTHOR

Jo Green prefers non gendered (they/them/their) pronouns. Jo started studying paganism in South Africa, their country of birth, in 2001 although they had studied of comparative religions prior to that. They joined a coven run by the Pagan Federation of South Africa in late 2002 where they completed initiate training. They left the coven for personal reasons.

Jo continued to study paganism in detailed and was privately tutored by their partner who was previously a member of the Pagan Federation of South Africa. In 2006 Jo and their partner started teaching and formed a much smaller more private coven with a number of friends who persisted in requesting training until they eventually conceded.

In 2008 the couple were presented with an opportunity to move to the United Kingdom, where they continue to teach in small groups to individual friends and run a small online group for trans pagans in the UK, a support group for couples where one person is transitioning and contribute to the local trans and pagan communities.

Made in the USA
Las Vegas, NV
15 May 2024

89979930R00102